# The SANE Economy

## Using ShareFlow Electronic Currency

### Alan Halverson

# ~ The SANE Economy ~

# The SANE Economy
Copyright© January 2018
by Alan R. Halverson

All Rights Reserved. No part of this book may be reproduced, stored in retrieval, or transmitted in any form, electronic, mechanical, or otherwise without the express consent of the author.

Library of Congress
Cataloging in Publication Data

ISBN-13:
978-1985783607
ISBN-10:
1985783606

*1st Edition*
*April 2018*

Published by
CreateSpace

Printed in the United States of America

All Truth is Relative and simply a Measure of one's Honest Perspective

# *Acknowledgements*

I wish to acknowledge all the unsung heroes of modern day economics, science and spiritual awakening far too numerous to mention in this presentation.

However, when the SANE Economy using ShareFlow Electronic Currency becomes a reality in the form of a viable force operating within a Network trending to emerge globally despite a hostile world environment, I will be more than happy to acknowledge names if I am still on Earth and able to so.

Mentioned by name or not, these individuals who have given me core ideas plus the impetus to write my perspective of An Idea Whose Time has surely arrived will be rewarded in many ways where value can never be measured with financial mathematics alone.

~ The SANE Economy ~

# CONTENTS

| | |
|---|---|
| Introduction | 8 |
| 1. ShareFlow Electronic Currency | 12 |
| 2. Non-Transferability | 20 |
| 3. The SANE Economic Model | 26 |
| 4. Creating an Abundance of Jobs | 36 |
| 5. Employment Matching | 44 |
| 6. Maintenance of ECU Accounts | 52 |
| 7. Expanding the ShareFlow Network | 58 |
| 8. Customer Ownership of the Banks | 68 |
| 9. Transparency of Operations | 74 |
| 10. Wage Allocations | 82 |
| 11. Debit for Products & Services | 90 |
| 12. Financial Accountability | 100 |
| 13. Government Cooperation | 106 |
| 14. The True Purpose of Money | 116 |
| 15. A Universal Monetary System | 124 |
| 16. The Self-Construct Economy | 130 |
| About the Author | 140 |

# Introduction

Imagine your ideal employment. You're a well-respected employee working for a company and management you love while doing the kind of work that makes your heart sing…

Now while you're doing your ideal thing, you get adequate pay for your needs, never have to pay any taxes and never have to worry about minor details like losing your job (guaranteed for life) or how much profit your company is making (your company isn't making any profit!)

Pie in the Sky?

It surely is now, but that Pie in the Sky is about to become Pie on your Plate!

Imagine that all you need for your personal purchase of anything (product or service) regardless of cost is a simple debit card tied to your account at your local bank.

As an employee of the business you love (including self-employment if you desire), you are also a customer for many businesses to purchase your essentials using only your debit card linked to your local bank.

No cash, checks, credit cards, or any other means of paying for something exists!... And that's a good thing!

Think for a moment…

There is a common definition of Socialism that always implies government control of the means of Production.

For any user-friendly economic policy to work as it should, there would be no government control on anyone…

Instead it would operate based upon local control and management of a Network of Local Banks owned by their Account Holders within each Local Banking District.

Collectively, all Account holders in any Banking District would be verified Employees of a qualified business and would own and control their own Local Bank and means of creating money for distribution as Employee Wages and Savings.

Welcome to the SANE Economy!

You're Welcome!

With SANE, money would be paid to every Employee working for any legitimate business within their District. using a *new kind of money* different from traditional standard currencies that can get sidetracked and used for political gain.

Let us define the distribution mechanism for this kind of money as **ShareFlow** (the practical distribution and flow of money created electronically and residing only in the Accounts within the *ShareFlow Network of Local Banks* operating under ShareFlow guidelines).

These Banks would create money as needed for Wage Allocations and pay it out to Account holders regardless of who they work for as long as their business is legitimate.

The basic responsibilities of **SANE**, otherwise known as: *The Socially Automated Network Economy* will be simple, straight-forward and well-defined in a Document known as the ShareFlow Constitution called **SANECon** to guide an internal staff dedicated for responsible operations.

That purpose of the first prototype Local Bank operation would be to *demonstrate the credibility* of what is possible to achieve in a full-fledged operation.

Ultimately it would take the place of all faulted economic policies by relying on a potential Universal Monetary System of earned currency that is equitably and adequately distributed as Wages to all who deserve compensation in return for their work that benefits the *Common Good*.

The Primary Directive of the SANE Economy would be to rely solely on a *unique* standard of electronic currency units so that the following objectives are maintained:

1 See that everyone gets paid adequately in Wages they deserve according to their responsible Employment Status and

2 See that everyone *pays a fair price* for all necessary products and services for themselves & families using only a personal Debit Card that would automatically subtract from their Wage/Savings Account for each specific purchase of any product or service.

Imagine getting paid adequately and automatically every payday while you are employed at the job you love, feel the most comfortable with and still have adequate free time to look for other opportunities in alternate employment if desired.

Imagine that your friends and even family members are also working in the business of their choice and are also getting paid automatically and adequately every regular payday so that everyone always has money in their Accounts to pay their bills.

Even though your friends and acquaintances may have chosen a variety of professions and jobs different from yours, all of you have two things in common.

Everyone would be given status as an Employee of a business that contributes to the **Common Good**, and each of us would have two personal Accounts in the same Local Bank, namely a ***Wage/Savings Account*** and a ***Purchase/Archive Account*** where they can work together for all transactions.

The money source is in the Local Bank itself where you and your friends and others living in your District would have their Bank Accounts set up indefinitely.

So how can the Local Banks pay ***everyone a fair wage?***

The answer – The money is not in dollars but in electronic currency units with a different designation – Let's call the new unit of money (author's choice) a Sharo.

What happens once Wages in Sharos are paid regularly to you and any responsible family members or friends who also have their Accounts at the Local Bank?

Answer: ***A worry-free budget experience for everyone.***

Wage money would automatically build up as Savings in the Wage/Savings Account each time Sharos are paid monthly (like Social Security).

Every Account holder in the Local Bank is also a consumer who could usually purchase their products and services within the community much like a communal organization will often buy locally produced products for consumption and trade.

What happens when Sharo electronic currency is spent in payment for a product or service?

Since all SANE money would be in the form of electronic currency only, there would be no checks, credit cards, cash, coins or other physical medium needed.

The result would be that no money leaves the Bank but simply gets transferred to the customer's Purchase/Archive Account to allow the Local Bank to keep track of everything purchased by all their customers within the District

All money remains in the Local Bank because when one uses their ShareFlow Debit Card for a purchase of either a product or a service, the business would *not* use or need that money since ***all their employees*** are auto-paid by ***their Bank*** as qualified by their Employee status in a reputable business.

All businesses would simply transfer the transaction details to the Local Bank where the cost of purchase in Sharos is subtracted from the Account Holder's Wage/Savings Account and put into their corresponding Purchase/Archive Account.

Everything about SANE officially defined as the Socially Automated Network Economy would be ***locally owned and driven by the ShareFlow Universal Monetary System***.

To be successful it must have two qualities that make most traditional systems of credit-clearing obsolete.

The first would be a basic understanding and willingness to cooperate by everyone who participates to make dynamics secure and reliable so that everyone benefits appropriately as in the premise of: ***Value Received for Value Earned***.

The second quality would be to use an exclusive and sensible currency based upon modern technological advances with electronic currency as the monetary standard and method used for an ***expanding Network of Local Banks.***

This my friends leads to Pure Economics as it should be using a well-designed ***Credit Clearing Process***.

Now read the details about how SANE and a ShareFlow Universal Monetary System could potentially work out to eventually go global in extent to benefit every man, woman and child on the face of the planet.

# ~1~
# ShareFlow Electronic Currency

All currency would be created directly by Local Banks within the ShareFlow Banking Network which would not accept or use any other source of money for transactions outside the ShareFlow System.

ShareFlow would exist and operate based only on getting money to those who deserve it and who are set up to accept all their income placed into a personal Wage/Savings Account.

These personal Accounts are set up to secure their monthly Wages in Sharos that represents the value of work they have done and are committed to continue to do to help contribute to the **Common Good**.

To be successful and secure, the ShareFlow System would create electronic currency in the form of **(whole number) Sharos** within each Local Bank as needed to pay out Wages.

ShareFlow could logically begin with only one Local Bank to eventually expand into a **ShareFlow Network**.

The Network would operate by exclusively using **Sharos** under **Local Control** and would have the potential to **expand globally** once all nations agree to commit to and support it.

No Sharos would be issued to anyone other than employed workers for businesses that have a proven track record of reliable service to the Common Good in their community.

All workers would apply for their Accounts exclusively located in the district in which they reside yet can access them anywhere in the world using the **ShareFlow Network** in much the same way as the larger banking networks already do with customers and their debit card linkage every day.

The major difference between ShareFlow and traditional banking would be that the Network would be set up so that no

# 1 ShareFlow Electronic Currency

money could be transferred to any other banking system, business corporation, government entity or individual person.

*The only outlay of Sharos would be in Wages* placed directly to all bank Account holders monthly that would never have to leave the Local Bank where the Accounts reside.

All ShareFlow Bank customers would be recognized as *"employees" working for any legitimate business or having self-employed status* who have earned their Wage payments and are authorized to continue to be paid a set amount at their level of value to the community at large.

As local banks prove successful in their operation with ShareFlow, the Network could eventually expand to include many more Local Banks and potentially become a *universal money standard based only on electronic currency*.

My suggestion for the name Sharo instead of the Dollar, the Euro or any other standard unit is because the name **Sharo** makes logical sense and could be psychologically suggestive of the *true purpose of money*.

Using Sharos, the ShareFlow Network could operate as an independent source of money for all participants having their Accounts with ShareFlow.

The ultimate goal would be to have all workers (worldwide) be given an appropriate Employee status, with autopay for their monthly Wages paid directly from their ShareFlow Local Bank instead of the business or profession they work for.

Even employees of the ShareFlow Local Banks themselves would be part of the System with individual access using personal *Wage/Savings and Purchase/Archive Accounts* residing within the same Local Bank where they work.

As such, they could *not have access to any money* other than what they earn as an Employee and are paid for in wages.

All Employees worldwide would be paid their appropriate Salary automatically from their own Local Bank that directly creates necessary allocations of Sharos for payment as Wages within their District.

Once the ShareFlow Network gains a foothold worldwide, all other traditional money could trend to obsolescence.

# 1 ShareFlow Electronic Currency

Since all money would be created as Sharos by each Local Bank in the Network, **no taxes of any kind** would be paid or required by anyone in the ShareFlow Network.

And since all workers are also consumers with specific needs, all products and services would be purchased only by the use of their **100% Non-Profit transactions** with personal Debit Cards accessing their Wage/Savings Accounts.

Because all workers would be paid adequately for doing whatever work their profession requires of them, the issue of affordable and adequate **Universal Single-Payer Healthcare** would be guaranteed to all at selected levels.

Everyone in the Network would have options to select whatever healthcare plan would be appropriate for their status as **employees** under the ShareFlow Monetary System.

The **first level of healthcare would be free to everyone** regardless of economic status because the concept of basic health as a human right would be automatically applied to keep everyone as healthy as possible in a stressful world.

Having ShareFlow as a sensible base for adequately created money for all with **no taxes or public debt** to worry about, a selection of other products and services could also be offered free of charge to the public due to technological advances making it possible for greater efficiency and quality of living regardless of economic status.

One of these services would be **free public education** for everyone at any age level from **kindergarten through the highest level of advanced education** throughout the world, because it would be accepted as a **human right**.

Whenever there are not enough educators, teachers and instructors, faculty or facilities to provide for universal free education, ShareFlow would increase or redirect money to pay for training the appropriate personnel to fill these positions and close any gaps that may occur.

Sharo money in **any transaction could be used only once and only by the person who they were issued to as Wages** in their Wage/Savings Accounts to be eventually used for purchases for necessary products and services.

# 1 ShareFlow Electronic Currency

All business transactions would transfer **used Sharos** to the customers' Local Banks where matching Purchase/Archive Accounts exist for each customer.

The results would be **simple transfers of the used money** from customer Wage/Savings Accounts to their appropriate Purchase/Archive Accounts.

All Products and Services worldwide would be value priced fairly and equitably so that no one would be inclined to waste time and energy looking for their "best" price on any given product or service.

Only Employment types for the **Common Good** would be supported by the ShareFlow Network.

For example, any employment involved with casinos, bartending, drug dealerships, gun manufacturers, distributers, or anything involved with the tobacco industry, alcoholic drinks, race track operations and certain sporting activities etc. **would not be supported**.

Instead, questionable industries like these could eventually be forced out of business with a universal monetary system such as ShareFlow focused only on the Common Good, and not for enabling opportunities to make **profit that people don't need nor have earned** to support the cause.

With carefully embedded and constitutionally mandated constraints, the ShareFlow Network would not allow these and similar businesses to be supported out of the best interests of everyone **including the former wealthy elite** who were once well-established in a culture of using their money only for self-interest or as a weapon to control others.

With ShareFlow, everyone could choose a type of work best suited for their need and be placed in a position that would best reflect their talents and mental state of what constitutes fulfillment in their lives.

To create more jobs and professions in line with demand and the Common Good, ShareFlow could have departments that monitor economic trends to **identify and prioritize all the professions and services where additional workers might be needed.**

# 1 ShareFlow Electronic Currency

ShareFlow money would be created on an as-needed basis whenever and wherever additional needs are identified.

Funding could either pay existing workers more to relocate to where the need is greatest or be used for education to hire additional faculty and support personnel to teach the skills and knowledge young people need to choose their professions.

In keeping with the Green Earth philosophy of using clean energy, ShareFlow would be committed to using only ***100% Renewable Clean Energy*** throughout the Network facilities in all operations around the world.

With the ShareFlow Network of Local Banks, no one could ever go into debt since debt could not exist in the way Sharo money would be managed by ShareFlow.

With ShareFlow working with SANE, all political money, poverty and virtually all homelessness would disappear since there would always be ***adequate and appropriate income*** for all responsible workers.

Anyone else who does not or cannot work for whatever reason would need to ***subsist on free sustenance basics*** for food, clothing, shelter and healthcare, or be paid with a ***minimum standard income*** for their specific needs in life.

All businesses and enterprises would be given adequate monetary support including all those that are proven to be contributors to the Common Good.

This would include all entrepreneurial efforts for new enterprises such as an invention, discovery, or relocation, etc.

Since the ShareFlow Network and operations would be owned by the customers of each Local Bank, there would always be a ***100% transparency*** offered to the public to come in at any time and examine all policies and procedures in the finest detail to assure that no fraudulent activity is involved.

A globalized Network of ShareFlow Banks would always maintain a continuous supply and a healthy flow of currency throughout a ***hypothetical 256 world nation state*** economy outlined on my website page entitled The SANG Government.

By disallowing any hoarding of funds by any individual, business, corporation or government, it could respond fairly, efficiently and proportionately to the needs of the entire extent of the world's population.

All currency and their accounts (worldwide) could reside within ShareFlow and never get side-tracked outside of the ShareFlow Network System.

Sharo electronic currency would be paid out at ShareFlow Local Banks to each of their local customer's Wage/Savings Accounts monthly to cover appropriate Wages, thus allocating payments appropriately to all responsible *employees* working for any approved company within their Local Bank District.

There would *never be any deficit or overspending* by anyone because ShareFlow would disallow any drift towards inflation, recession, depression or other economic imbalance and could eventually do away with the need for the IRS, the Federal Reserve and the Stock Market.

As a result, there would always be the correct amount of funding going to whoever needs and deserves it resulting from their *employment status* and thus would *be independent of profit* from any business, corporation or government.

There would be *no taxation of any type* at any level or at any time since there would always be an endless supply of new currency created and allocated by the ShareFlow Banking Network residing in each Local Bank.

***All social services would be provided for according to the priorities of human need.***

With ShareFlow, credit debt would never be extended or needed since the Network would automatically prevent anyone from going into debt.

Everyone participating within the ShareFlow Network would be compensated adequately for all useful work rendered no matter what their station in life would be.

Universal ShareFlow Wages and Accounts would be all-encompassing and comprehensive in a system that could work efficiently by *automating all global monetary transactions exclusively for earning and spending.*

Instead of credit cards or checkbooks, the Network would automate transactions using electronic currency in the form of

# 1 ShareFlow Electronic Currency

Sharos, and then archive the used money within the Local Bank from which they were created.

All spent units would be salvaged for economic trending analysis in appropriate Purchase/Archive Accounts belonging to the customers that used them for their personal needs.

As such, Sharos would be used only once for a transaction.

Every citizen could own one or more personal **Account monitors** and a ShareFlow **Account Debit Card** replacing all cash, credit cards, coins and check books, etc. for **subtracting the cost of purchases from their Wage/Savings Account** in a manner similar to how any debit card is used today.

But in ShareFlow operations, the customer's Sharos are deducted from their Wage/Savings Account and transferred to their corresponding Purchase/Archive account in their Local Bank that deactivates them from further circulation.

Archived Sharos would be stored and eventually analyzed for research and development of trending economic activities.

Each business doing a transaction for a purchase by any customer would have only one financial responsibility in sales no matter what the products or services would be.

That purpose is to make sure each transfer of customer funds to a Local Bank is efficient, accurate and secure.

Businesses would **no longer have to keep track of profit**, and could thrive automatically since **all their employees could also be paid adequately by ShareFlow** in regular monthly Wage transactions.

ShareFlow and other sub-divisions of the SANE Economy would use redundant backup capabilities and foolproof code transactions to disallow any possibility of hacking in Accounts.

Every transaction would be recorded with code numbers of both buyer and seller and would be **redundantly available throughout all Local Banks in the ShareFlow Network** that could operate securely to eliminate any error or attempted hacking from any source.

The fundamental concept of the SANE Economy would be based upon the simple supposition that whoever deserves a specific amount of money (Sharos) receives it; and whoever

# 1 ShareFlow Electronic Currency

does not deserve any specific allocation of money will not get it until they earn it and are set up to earn it legitimately.

Within the ShareFlow Network, ***all electronic currency being strictly Non-Transferable***, would disallow any funds leaking into politics or corporate control through investments, interest, leverage or other non-productive means.

Since ShareFlow would be owned, operated, managed and controlled only by the Shareholders (the people who hold ShareFlow Accounts and use their Local Bank for all their financial transactions), the entire operations of ShareFlow and The SANE Economy could and would remain fully secure and transparent to any citizen who feels it necessary to monitor security and fairness of operations.

# ~2~
# Non-Transferability

For the ShareFlow Network, **Non-Transferability** is the quality of allowing electronic currency to be issued *only from a Local Bank in the Network* that would disallow any possession by anyone except the intended recipient for purposes of saving, ownership or purchase of goods and services.

With ShareFlow, the aspect of non-transferability is crucial, and the core requirement that the Local Banks of the Network must commit to and be responsible to maintain in order that ShareFlow Money (Sharos) would be *issued only as Wages to responsible Wage Earners*.

Recipients of Sharos would only be workers that qualify for Wages in the Bank District where they reside or operate from and would likewise be *disallowed to transfer any of it to another individual, business, corporation or government facility.*

Every dispensation of money created by the Local Banks would be intended for use only by a designated and responsible worker of any qualified business in the Bank District or one of their dependent family members.

Each recipient is recognized as an Employee of a qualified business and would receive Sharos automatically as their Wages in a Bank held Wage/Savings Account that can be used only by that Employee or dependent family member.

Once taken out of an Employee's Account *(with a Debit Card used for a purchase of a product or service), these used Sharos would be deactivated for further use.*

Instead, they would simply be transferred to the *employee's* Purchase/Archive Account of spent money so that it becomes part of their record of purchases for budget analysis and a record of current trends in the local economy at the Local Bank.

## 2 Non-Transferability

The purpose of archiving would thus be two-fold.

By taking used money out of circulation so it could not be fraudulently transferred as active currency to another individual, business, corporation or government account, it would be on record for the Network to help keep track of *economic trends in Wages and purchases* throughout the global economy.

This same procedure would be used for every Employee who has their Accounts at their Local Bank so that it results in having all responsible workers receive Wage money directly from their Local Bank on a regular schedule each month.

All purchase transactions would be recorded automatically with a ShareFlow Debit Card that accesses the worker's personal Wage/Savings Account and completes the transaction with an auto-transfer of the Sharo cost of each purchase to the worker's Purchase/Archive Account and taking it out of circulation.

The combination of *Local Bank Management, Control and Creation of all* money within the ShareFlow Network together with the aspect of *non-transferability* means that no funds could get away from the intended source or target of disbursement to fall into the wrong hands for fraudulent or adverse control purposes.

Result: *No taxes* would ever need to be paid or needed and *no taxes* could ever be collected by anyone or entity since there would always be an endless supply of new money in Sharos created as needed by each Local Bank.

With adequate security measures put into place, this transfer of money remaining within each Bank amounts to *only two simple operations to make the System work well for all:*

*1.* Newly created electronic currency in Sharos would be put into a Local Bank Master Account and auto-transferred to each registered Wage/Savings Account as a monthly allocation paid *to each responsible Employee of any business in the Local District where they are employed.*

*2.* Whenever a Bank customer within a Local District has accessed their Wage/Savings Account for purchasing something of value be it a product or service, the corresponding cost of the

## 2 Non-Transferability

transaction is moved out of their Wage/Savings Account and into their Purchase/Archive Account as deactivated currency.

This simple two-fold responsibility of ShareFlow assures that no money would get into the hands of anyone with illicit motives such as criminals, politicians, corporate heads or anyone else who wants to hoard money or misuse it for their own purposes.

Regarding charities, many responsible folks are willing to donate to help others in our present day and age in a manner reflecting what they think they can afford.

**With ShareFlow, all charities would become obsolete** since the financial well-being of previous recipients of charity would be handled in other ways to guarantee that their subsistence needs are adequately provided.

If the kindness of charity-minded folks demands an outlet, they can offer food and other commodities as gifts directly to bypass the usual method of donating money since monetary donations through ShareFlow would no longer be allowed.

One issue that comes to mind is how does ShareFlow Wage allocations operate when there is a new birth or an adoption of a child into a family?

Whenever there is a newborn or an adopted child coming into a household, that family would need extra income to cover the additional expense.

ShareFlow would be set up to provide additional money to a responsible family member (mother or father) and would be reflected as an *increase in monthly payments for each newborn, adopted child or even a new family pet.*

In fact, ShareFlow could even support extra money to all those who *adopt pets in a responsible manner*, while the SANE Economic model would follow up with adequate funds to *cover reasonable veterinary expenses* as an add-on to normal Wage allotments.

The SANECon Constitution mandated rule for the SANE Economy and ShareFlow however would be that no funding would be created, dispensed or transferred to anyone other than existing workers who earns it.

# 2 Non-Transferability

Anyone else responsible for the caring of a newborn would be given the status of an Employee so that newborns could be identified in the ShareFlow System as needing to be covered financially by a responsible adult who would have adequate income via their individual Employee status.

When a child becomes of age to have an *Employee status set up as a student* to receive income and have their own Debit Card for purchases, the Local Bank issues them their Card and sets up their non-transferable money Account to be adjusted accordingly as long as the student remains responsible and attends school as expected.

In a similar manner, the parent's Wage/Savings Account is adjusted downward by the same amount that is no longer needed to support a dependent when their child reaches adult status to be on their own financially.

In the case of a death in the family, that person's account would be deleted, and no more money would be allocated.

If necessary, there could be a one-time additional allocation put into the Wage/Savings Account of whoever is responsible for funeral expenses as a dispensation of *common-right death expense*, since it would be offered to all families experiencing a death and needing that kind of help.

Since ShareFlow money could not be transferred to any other person or entity, it means that *all political money would cease except for responsible campaign expenses* residing in the personal accounts of politicians and candidates running for any office at any level in government.

Result: All politicians already holding public office would be constrained to use only *a reasonable amount of money they already have in their Accounts due to employment status*, plus any extra they qualify for to meet appropriate expenses in handling their total campaign costs.

For those running to unseat incumbents, an appropriate *standard amount of additional funds* could be allocated for their *employment status to advertise their message and credentials to public view* so that the voters could get an accurate and clear message to compare between candidates.

## 2 Non-Transferability

All candidates running for offices would be **held to the constraints of equitable funding** for all campaign-related costs and would need to use their additional Wage allocations via ShareFlow to advertise their credentials and personal resume using only reasonable campaign expenses.

There would be no money allowed to filter in to lobbyists, corporations, or any other source to try to tip the balance in favor of any candidate regardless of what party they represent or how popular they are in the eyes of the public.

Bottom line: There would be constraints to maintain **100% financial fairness in all elections at all levels** because ShareFlow money would act as the Universal Standard and be allocated based only on accepted **employment status**.

Regarding the types of employment that would cease or be unsupported by ShareFlow, we can include gambling, so-called vice-related activities for monetary profit, illegal drug dealing, horse and dog racing, violent or dangerous sporting activities and the production and distribution of weapons, etc.

Also unsupported would be anything to do with weapons other than qualified simple types designed for the police, some military personnel and basic citizen self-defense.

Harmful industries such as alcoholic drink production and distribution, the tobacco industry, investment brokers, violent sporting activities and anything traditionally associated with the **profit motive** will not be supported.

The primary benefit of the non-transferable aspect of ShareFlow would be **the virtual elimination of crime based upon fraudulent monetary gain of any type**.

It would no longer be possible for anyone (criminal or otherwise) to rob, steal, extort or plunder for money of any type because ordinary transferable forms of money would no longer exist with ShareFlow for monetary disbursement.

Any attempt to defraud a person with only their ShareFlow Debit Card could not work either because there would be adequate security measures put in place to simply disallow any type of transfer of funds from one person's account to another electronically or otherwise.

## 2 Non-Transferability

Identity Theft would not be possible because of ***adequate security measures*** and the official policy of how money is dispensed as Wages only and Debited as Purchases only would be handled and become common knowledge.

Any potential thief would likely not try to commit a crime for money out of common knowledge that it would not work.

With ShareFlow, any criminal mind would be faced with a virtually impossible task of trying to get around security due to redundant layers of checks and balances put in place.

Those that might want to defraud the System ***might not have much motivation or incentive to do so anyway*** since they would generally be getting their own adequate money through legitimate means in an enjoyable non-profit type of work doing the things they love with no time or energy left to focus on crime.

# ~3~
# The SANE Economic Model

I see the SANE Economic Model as inclusive but not limited to the following eight major components which must work in tandem to obtain the SANE objectives:

1. Universal ShareFlow Currency
2. Universal Renewable Clean Energy
3. Universal Free Public Education
4. Universal Fair Expense Pricing
5. Universal Fair Income Limits
6. Universal Comprehensive Insurance
7. Universal Capital & Job Creation
8. Universal Employment Matching

## Universal ShareFlow Currency

For initial startup of the SANE Economy, a prototype Local Bank using *only dedicated ShareFlow currency called Sharos* would need to be set up and offer to *create personal Accounts for qualified workers including the employees of the Bank and other workers employed at other qualified businesses* in the Local Bank District).

Everyone having an Account set up with their Local Bank would be given official status as an Employee, but

## 3 The SANE Economic Model

not necessarily employed by the Bank, but be working for any responsible business in the District that supports and works with the ShareFlow Banking System.

No one would ever need or use a credit card, cash, coins, checkbook or other physically visible forms of money.

***No one would ever pay taxes*** of any kind since all the required currency for circulation would be created within the ShareFlow Local Banking Network.

All purchases would be recorded, secured and handled electronically with a ShareFlow Debit Card much the same as ordinary debit cards already do with traditional accounts, but no other monetary operations would be needed or allowed.

## Universal Renewable Clean Energy

SANE would commit to basing all operations on their ***Universal Renewable Clean Energy (URCE)*** System by selecting the best combinations of solar, wind, hydrogen storage or other clean energy method that can be integrated as a coordinated system for operations around the clock.

In many areas around the world, bank facilities could source their energy requirements solely from the wind using an array of **vertical axis wind turbine generators** together with using **electrolysis of water** for hydrogen storage or battery backup.

In other areas, a combination of Solar Array Systems (SAS) and Wind Turbine Systems (WTS) could be used to achieve the same goal, while in still other localities, a SAS System alone might be the best and only requirement.

Standard modular units for either SAS or WTS of various capacities could adjust to a variety of climate/latitude differences for best performance and could be modified as needed when climate change occurs locally.

In situations where climate is unpredictable or where calm winds and cloudy days happen to predominate, larger or alternate combinations of SAS and WTS systems could logically be used in modular units and be mass produced and distributed for best cost effectiveness.

# 3 The SANE Economic Model

Integrated solar and wind energy power plants could also be operated successfully on the open seas which could be alternately designed for fixed or mobile functionality.

Ocean-based power plants could likely be set up to not only power their operations, but to **specialize in hydrogen fuel storage production** for transport to land based users.

For the homeowner, standardized WTS setups will likely be used that feature arrays of vertical axis turbines instead of horizontal axis units.

**Vertical axis types can operate in a wide range of wind speeds and directions** as well as being more pleasing to the eye and less intrusive to the environment.

They could be **designed for maximum efficiency in average wind conditions, operational at low and high wind speeds, and have a speed cutoff capability for maximum rotational velocity** as protection in damaging winds.

Each turbine could be set up with an AC conversion module, enabling direct conversion to consumer needs.

Linear alternators could also be used and have advantages of simple design, greater efficiency, compactness, and constant frequency AC power output.

In similar fashion, SAS solar setups could be standardized, modularized, and power rated with respect to variable sunlight conditions such as locality and time of year usage.

Using electrolysis to produce stored hydrogen could also be used to produce a combination system for maximum efficiency I would refer to as an SWHS for an integrated solar, wind and hydrogen storage system.

For rural areas, an SWHS would most likely be needed to provide dependable and reliable electrical power for various uses approaching 24/7 efficiency.

In many cases, it also could provide hydrogen fuel or battery power for a family automobile as a supplementary benefit.

**Homeowners could choose how many modules of each type would work best for their situation**, considering climate, latitude, terrain, aesthetics and home energy requirements.

# 3 The SANE Economic Model

For the cold windless nights of winter in moderate and high latitudes, a logical choice for a storage system would need to use a reliable backup to supply heat as necessary.

Each SWHS could include a complete climate control system and facilities for maintaining *a small greenhouse* to grow and supply produce for homeowners and their families.

Climate control units would include central heating and air conditioning, air filtering and ionization control and humidity balance for home and greenhouse compatibility.

All SWHS Systems could be designed as modules for easy use by homeowners, farmers and businesses for purchase and installation of only the number, type & size of units needed.

As technology advances, we will likely have one more source of renewable clean energy to consider that is not talked about much but could potentially become the *ultimate clean energy source* that would be superior to all the others.

This is ZPE (Zero Point Energy) which will have many advantages over solar and wind as a 100% renewable and clean source as soon as available technology makes the conversion process accessible to public knowledge.

Basic practical use would consist of a collection of metal containers that have certain *wave transformation equipment embedded inside* to convert *high energy and high-frequency background radiation impinging at any point in space* to electricity for storage in high-efficiency batteries.

The over-riding *advantage of zero-point* is that ZPE converters could be placed *anywhere* (such as inside or outside a building) and could continuously extract energy *at any point independent of location* once the technology is perfected.

The most important advantage of ZPE is that the energy could be extracted independently of solar, wind, or directional placement, and potentially become the *ultimate free energy for anything electricity is used for.*

The potential for practical use would be enormous, and the technology to make it accessible continues despite intense political pressures that try to shut it down in favor of fossil fuels.

# 3 The SANE Economic Model

## Universal Free Public Education

SANE would use a *Universal Free Public Education (UFPE) Program* to cover all reasonable costs to enable Free Public Education at all levels.

It could include housing, tuition, books, lab equipment and any other costs *not covered by student employment status.*

ShareFlow could automatically pay Wages to Employed teachers, professors and all faculty support personnel to maintain free public education for all responsible students throughout all their public education experience.

ShareFlow and SANE could assure that necessary supplies are always available for all school facilities and that new job openings are created as needed to provide new employment to fill vacancies as required for expanding schools and facilities.

They would also commit to assure that adequate *teaching methods at all class levels are planned for, supported and adequately funded* in the form of *auto-paid job openings* in all categories of necessary personnel.

## Universal Fair Expense Pricing

Another important feature of the SANE Economy would be the *Universal Fair Expense Pricing (UFEP) Program* to assure that all purchases of products and services will be based upon fair value exchange.

Once determined, these standards would remain relatively fixed to avoid disruptions of inflation and recessions, etc.

With UFEP, any customer would pay about the same fixed costs with only minor adjustments if needed.

A typical consumer purchasing any product anywhere in the world would no longer want to use coupons or look for special deals because purchase costs would tend to be about the same at every location.

In a similar manner, any purchase for services would tend to cost about the same independent of location.

# 3 The SANE Economic Model

Comparison shopping of either products or services would *depend only on factors different from cost*, such as quality of products or services rendered.

Comparison shopping could use the capitalistic principle of competition to ensure high quality control, but in a different manner independent of money-saving offers or of businesses always attempting to bring in greater profit.

*It would rely solely on customer satisfaction involving quality of products, attitudes of sales personnel and track records of reliability* in merchandizing, etc.

## Universal Fair Income Limits

All welfare programs would be replaced gradually with a *Universal Fair Income Limits (UFIL) Program.*

This would include the provision that every man, woman and child on Earth should eventually have an *unconditional income intended for food, clothing, shelter and the basics of healthcare* regardless of being employed or not employed.

Any income above and beyond that would *need to be earned* by useful employment helping the *Common Good*.

Equal allocations would be given to everyone working or not, but would be accompanied with positive incentives to contribute to the support for free acquisition.

With SANE Economic concepts in operation, virtually everyone could find a favorable job opportunity of reasonable contributory value in a type of work they would love to do.

Because of that, most citizens would be more than happy to support a *sensible welfare state* that would work very well for the *unemployed as well as for the under-employed* at all levels of income.

This mandate would be fair to all because every employed worker would get a *base minimum income plus salary*, while the unemployed for whatever reason would receive only their *base minimum income without salary* and would have to use only that income to live on.

# 3 The SANE Economic Model

Non-transferable ECUs would operate in such a way as to disallow use of one's Wage allocations for anything except for saving and purchasing qualified necessities of life.

On the other end of the Income Spectrum, appropriate upper limit caps on Wage/Savings Accounts for Wages, Salaries and Net-Worth would also be set appropriately by ShareFlow and SANE and defined according to their individual Employee status such that anyone's attempt to accumulate money beyond reasonable limits would be disallowed.

To operate properly, all subsystems of SANE will need to be networked together in conjunction with a new form of government that could logically be referred to as the Socially Automated Network Government (SANG).

And with all SANE Economic subsystems working together in complete cooperation, the result would be *the elimination of all antiquated money concepts that have enslaved humanity for untold generations*.

ShareFlow would be constrained to disallow the possibility of acquiring funds that are not legitimate, since all transactions would be secured and qualified as legitimate.

All transactions would need to be logically and redundantly validated without any concern that the System would be compromised in any significant manner.

Therefore, any transaction including all Wage payments, product and service purchases could be traced to all individuals involved in the transactions.

Fortunately, it is human nature for most people to strive for the finer things in life in an honest manner.

Keeping that in mind, the motivation to better oneself through a reasonable effort would always tend to be the rule and not the exception.

With SANE in operation, *the likely tendency would be to favor honest transactions* instead of looking for ways to take advantage of others fraudulently.

Most everyone of average intelligence can understand that raising one's standard of living should involve reasonable

## 3 The SANE Economic Model

effort and a willingness to contribute to the benefit of everyone without interfering in the rights and freedoms of others.

Logic should dictate that when everyone cooperates with a reasonable economic effort, everyone can enjoy the advantages of higher standards of living.

An evolving ShareFlow Banking Network and their Local Bank Managing Teams will need to research all means of qualified employment to assure that all Wages are set in a fair manner irrespective of location, race, gender or station in life.

All applicable factors regarding fair earnings for each job description would be submitted for analysis.

Even menial task laborers could then earn as much as the head of a corporation if their effort put forth turned out to be of approximately equal value to Society.

*Factors such as benefits to society, responsibilities, productivity, work energy, skills and job hazards could all be considered for evaluation.*

Elected officials, corporate heads, and other management positions would be limited to predetermined Wages, Salaries and other compensations in like manner, based upon the total picture of all their pertinent value considerations.

*Within SANE, pay scales would no longer depend upon who you know, or what strings you can pull, or what ethnic background or gender you happen to be.*

Based upon a complete value-analysis, each job description would be assigned fair ShareFlow Wage payments in Sharos.

## Universal Comprehensive Insurance

Within SANE, a *Universal Comprehensive Insurance (UCI) Program* could include the whole gamut of insurance needs including accident, life, health, unemployment, disability, property damage, loss of income, etc.

This Program would abolish all the wasted effort, red tape and hassling typical of virtually all the competitive plans in existence that are controlled by profit motivation.

# 3 The SANE Economic Model

With much greater efficiency, the UCI Program would no longer have to account for who is covered and who is not, or what is covered and what is not.

When natural disasters and other global catastrophes are at a minimum, there would be more ShareFlow funds set aside for the less impacting insurance considerations.

***UCI would commit to be efficiently organized in order to eliminate all other forms of insurance and disaster aid.***

As a universal unemployment insurance covering anyone in true need, UCI would likely reduce crime everywhere by phasing out the ranks of the excessively poor.

It would likely provide opportunities for countless millions to tap into their true talents by allowing them time to secure optimum employment without undue stress.

On a prioritized basis, UCI would cover losses from every natural disaster such as with floods, tornadoes, earthquakes, fires, droughts, etc. and consequently would eliminate the need for separate disaster relief.

As part of SANE, UCI would be organized to facilitate all qualified compensation with fair and equitable treatment for everyone on a priority schedule operating in a hierarchy of legitimate human need.

## Universal Capital & Job Creation

The ***Universal Capital & Job Creation*** (***UCJC***) System would be another vital part of the SANE Economy.

It would allocate necessary funds as Wages to workers to create new jobs for businesses, schools and corporations with entrepreneurial opportunities.

It would also support expansion plans to increase selection and quality of products and services or to provide training for new employees in existing enterprises.

It would be designed to help maintain a vigorous and sustainable funding to support Education at all levels from kindergarten on up and be the prime incentive to target all the priorities of Public Education to identify new job creation.

# 3 The SANE Economic Model

These would include not only traditional math, science and engineering programs needed for the practical building blocks of society, but even more importantly, the social programs needed to insure, maintain and treat mental health, provide freedom from drug abuse, and teach young people the skills needed to interact in a responsible manner with their peers and fellow citizens when they become adults.

*The UCA would automatically provide necessary funding for the most promising clean energy cutting-edge technologies that need full development and introduction to the public for mass production.*

If an invention, discovery or expansion of an existing business can be validated as a beneficial contribution to the Common Good, it would be given adequate financial support.

## Universal Employment Matching

The *Universal Employment Matching (UEM)* System would need to be part of SANE in order to locate, identify and match job s with the best employment opportunities for all professions currently available anywhere around the world.

Even though SANE would be designed specifically for the Economy, it is likely that the benefits of better employment choices would spill over to strengthen all the social and cultural institutions in many ways that could unify all social structures.

*The goal of UEM would be to keep everyone who is willing and able to work employed in the most optimum positions offered for their skills, talents and personality.*

Whenever a job or position of employment is phased out, UEM would be there to immediately offer the job many new and even better employment opportunities.

With these eight systems of SANE in full development and working together with ShareFlow as the Universal Monetary System, the stage will be set for a potential Global Economy that would work consistently well for every man, woman and child on the face of the planet.

# ~4~
# Creating an Abundance of Jobs

The SANE commitment to a New Economy would be based upon a prime directive: (A social-needs focus to ultimately match a simultaneous creation of jobs with money **to support all necessary employment (universal and global in scope)**.

It could be a startup commitment beginning with only one Local Bank and supporting SANE Economics to match money creation with the costs of all the products and services the Local District could have available for purchase with Sharos.

In other words, support money and jobs would be created simultaneously by ShareFlow and SANE so that reliance upon creating jobs outside the System would be avoided to remain focused on social needs rather than business profits.

This is exactly opposite to our economic tradition of using government-created money operating in an uncontrolled miasma to try to maximize profits of business and corporations.

Obviously, it is a monumental disservice to take money out of the economy needed by the average citizen to support the interests of the political and wealthy elite.

For any economic model, especially a new one of potentially universal ramifications, there is a moral responsibility to direct all new and improved positions of employment to where it is most needed in order to support the cherished values required for the benefit of the ***Common Good***.

The ***Prime Directive of SANE*** would be a ***focus on social needs First*** so that everyone globally could ultimately benefit in an adjustable and self-improving system over time instead of a self-destruct system we are all slaves to at present.

In doing so, it must be able to sustain itself through adequate employment creation and maintain a database of numerous job opportunities whenever and wherever needed.

# 4 Creating an Abundance of Jobs

It must also maintain an efficient way to give all potential job-s the incentive to accept relocation or training if necessary to fill the best professional employment positions available according to priority needs.

It could give incentives for existing manpower to accept the challenges and opportunities that go along with the priority jobs wherever they exist to produce and successfully deliver the products and services their positions of employment are designed to offer.

In return, **SANE and ShareFlow will compensate all new and existing job holders everywhere** for committing to the challenges and opportunities that priority employment might entail and are available in any location in the world.

ShareFlow would need to guarantee adequate income in the form of Sharo electronic currency auto-transferred into all Employee Wage/Savings Accounts by their Local Banks and taken out as required to pay for any and every purchase of products and services.

SANE would not follow the traditional formula of opening new jobs whenever profits allow because all companies would operate in non-profit status.

***The mandated rules for ShareFlow and SANE to follow as described in the SANECon Constitution would disallow financial support for any jobs created outside the ShareFlow Network.***

SANE would not be dependent on profit because it would create all the money needed at each Local Bank for patrons in their District and have their Accounts with ShareFlow.

Instead SANE would employ a more powerful driving force called focusing on the social and subsistence needs to complete fulfillment of all work required to deliver products and services intended for the Common Good.

The SANE Economy will need to address this important issue with their subsystem: Universal Capital & Job Creation (***UCJC***) (which in theory could have offices located within each Local Bank separate from those used by ShareFlow to create Sharo ECU dispensation for Wages.

# 4 Creating an Abundance of Jobs

Since Local Banks would have full control of the SANE Economic Model and monetary supply, it would be logical to give SANE authority for Employment Creation to compete with traditional job creation.

Traditional job creation by CEOs of corporations and the financial heads of a business or government seemingly struggle for more money to fill adequate job creation because they are obviously locked into the ***need for profit*** to do so.

With advances in technology and greater awareness of our moral responsibilities, that is no longer a cool way to operate.

Instead, all necessary decisions and logistics could better be accomplished within the ranks of the ShareFlow Network on a Local Bank level to demonstrate the better way.

Specifically, each Local Bank could include an In-House partition of ***UCJC*** called the ***ShareFlow Employment Identification Service*** (SEIS).

SEIS would be responsible for identifying shortages in manpower, and thus could monitor local, national and even international needs for new employment of all types in real-time modes of operation.

A special communication network of websites could act as a universal employment creation entity with priority emphasis on local job and professional service needs.

The specific function of SEIS would be to monitor the pulse of economic activity and new growth opportunities so that ShareFlow could add to the creation of Wage Allocation Money to meet new employment demands within each district.

As SEIS begins to identify shortages of manpower to meet each specific demand within their community, the local SEIS offices would put out official notices in the ShareFlow Network of jobs currently available in real time.

This would give all potential manpower ready for hire anywhere in the world and participating in the ShareFlow Network the opportunity to apply for specific openings and consider relocation if necessary to better their own situation and help fulfill priority employment needs.

# 4 Creating an Abundance of Jobs

For purposes of the following examples, let us assume that a local SEIS Office would eventually exist in each ShareFlow Local Bank District within the ShareFlow Network.

Aside from air, water is the next basic physical need for our existence anywhere in the world.

And since water dependency is an obvious need for greater employment in many parts of the world to supply that need, it has the potential to generate many job opportunities that so far have been neglected due to the usual culprit: lack of funds.

In some parts of the world, water is fresh, abundant and economical for drinking purposes.

As rainfall it is adequately available in many places for agricultural needs, however the *opposite is true in many other locations* that used to have regular rain and snow melt.

Since water is of such high priority to sustain all humans and other life forms, there is obviously a high-priority need to direct new employment opportunities to every location where water is critically scarce.

Traditional economics mandates that loans are not always available to enable workers to get to the drought-stricken areas and find innovative ways to bring adequate and critical water supplies to the people that need them the most.

With SANE there would be no problem, since *money would be created as needed within any ShareFlow Local Bank to hire new workers* to respond to the additional need of sourcing water and getting it delivered to each area where it is critically short on supply.

Another example of new employment and job creation requirements facing much of the world today is in the vast field of **Renewable Clean Energy (RCE).**

Since SANE itself would always be committed to RCE anywhere and everywhere in the world, each SEIS Office based within the Network could identify locations where Clean Energy facilities, equipment and personnel can give it the robust support it needs to expand operations.

***Solar and wind energy conversion systems alone can account for an exceptionally rapid demand*** as well as an

## 4 Creating an Abundance of Jobs

increase in research facilities, production locations, distribution and delivery equipment.

SANE would fully support education and training of those who would accept hire with appropriate companies to install and maintain the conversion systems.

All steps in the process would require more trained employees to bring any combination of clean energy systems to homes and businesses in most locations throughout the world that still lack development and continue to rely mostly on fossil fuel production.

A typical SEIS Office *located within each Local Bank of the ShareFlow Network could monitor online requests for RCE* and set up specific-need profiles according to input from locations requesting support.

It would be responsible to determine how many new job openings would be needed to cover all work requests after the required documentation has been received and reviewed to qualify legitimate needs.

Once all information has been processed, specific job offers would be set up to post online so that potential job s could research and review for comparison.

They could set up their own profile to match their interests, education and skills to the posted requirements for each job opening they are interested in applying for.

Alternately, all those interested in applying for any new type of work could submit an all-encompassing resume to see which openings might best match their skills and interests.

*Using the latter case as in a shotgun approach, the job applicant can expect to receive an extensive slew of responses that cover potentially many areas of expertise they might never have thought about on their own.*

For example, in applying for a job anywhere in the Renewable Clean Energy field, there would likely be a huge list including some research positions specifying **workable zero-point applications** that use portable units to tap into energy from the universal ether of ultra-high frequency vibrations existing in ordinary cosmic background radiation.

# 4 Creating an Abundance of Jobs

If a job applicant has the skills, education and interest in this growing field of the *ultimate in clean energy*, it is quite possible that some applicants would be guided into this area through SANE Employment Matching.

One thing for sure is that with the SEIS offices of SANE creating new jobs whenever and wherever they are most needed, most applicants would likely come across extensive opportunities they might not have thought existed.

As a result, they would find an excellent matchup out of a variety of choices at all levels of the socio-economic spectrum.

**It is likely that SEIS would always be able to create more new jobs than existing job s at all times.**

Another area of potentially explosive growth would be in agriculture and related food production and distribution industries using controlled greenhouse food sources.

The advantages of greenhouse growing are obvious and inherently exist in most any location where extensive farming is not tenable due to toxic pesticide usage, high costs of food delivery, scarcity of dependable water supplies and lack of environmental control over production.

The advantages of employing **Controlled Environmental Greenhouse (CEG) usage would include an increase in the abundance and variety of many common food items.**

This method is critically important for food production in many parts of the world now isolated from consistent supply due to politics and climate change.

CEG usage alone has the potential to change the world in the way food is produced, guaranteed fresh and delivered to most any locality urban or rural where affordable supplies and quality of produce is hard to come by.

Another example of additional employment need is in the creation and distribution of **Easily Transportable Mobile & Motor Homes** to respond quickly when and where needed.

Prior to predicted disaster hits, the needs are crucial such as in hurricanes, floods and fire prone areas.

Residents in potential danger areas like these could quickly and efficiently evacuate in an orderly and controlled manner.

# 4 Creating an Abundance of Jobs

These mobile units could enable residents to load up and take with them irreplaceable valuables including their pets to avoid heartaches or injuries that could likely occur if residents are blind-sided by a weather or man-made disaster.

*A simple motor home evacuation technique could be set up in strategic locations near where potential disasters such as these often occur* and are seen as becoming more common place at the time of this writing.

*Well-organized master-plans of using mass-produced mobile homes could provide new employment for many in production, distribution, and vehicle maintenance.*

These jobs could be self-perpetuating with new employees filling job vacancies on an ongoing 24/7 basis.

The SEIS offices of ShareFlow would be set up to offer services and money in Sharos created by the ShareFlow Local Bank to support these requirements.

*For Vehicular Production and Distribution in general,* new or existing employment could be quickly identified to set up more availability for new cars, trucks and other vehicles designed to *use only clean energy sources*.

Existing technologies could be taught to trainees as part of Trade School agendas using SEIS job openings and ShareFlow money to finance whatever would be needed to expand vehicle manufacturing and distribution.

As always, ShareFlow and SANE would support only a 100% commitment to use renewable clean energy sources for every level of operation to avoid any use of fossil fuels.

In the *Nutritional Food and Supplement Industries*, openings for new employment could be offered in areas most conducive to *easy access to the source locations* for greater production and distribution efficiency.

Aside from local market food production, consideration could also target global outlets for easy and less expensive transport to famine and drought-stricken areas.

To help *Growth in Science and New Technologies*, SEIS could easily respond to requests online for more capital

## 4 Creating an Abundance of Jobs

to pay for foreign and domestic entrepreneurships that often go wanting for lack of financial support.

For space exploration, new research in ***zero-point energy conversion, anti-gravity and other science*** involving new sources for energy would be fully supported.

ShareFlow could support new facilities to encourage and expand more ambitious space-travel with smart research and experimentation that can only succeed by unfettering all limits on responsible financial support.

It could also enable a more balanced budget approach to support discoveries beyond our present understanding that in the end would clearly benefit the Common Good.

Within the ShareFlow and SANE operational offices, there would be an ongoing need to fill new positions expeditiously as the Network expands operations and responds to periodic vacancies under one roof wherever practical.

It would mean that all in-house employment openings within ShareFlow and other offices supporting SANE could be easily identified and filled quickly with qualified personnel who could accept on-the-job training.

Once SEIS completes work on ***job identification*** with their postings of all current job openings local and otherwise, the next step in the process would be handled by the SANE Employment Matching Service referred to as SEMS.

## ~5~
## Employment Matching

Working with the ShareFlow Employment Identification Service SEIS, another closely related sub-system would be the logical add-on to operate within ShareFlow called the ***SANE Employment Matching Service (SEMS).***

This subsystem could be a sophisticated and far-reaching online-support effort associated and communicating directly with the ***ShareFlow banking Network.***

SEMS would be responsible to match all job applicants with their best professional opportunities showing up in real-time and needing satisfying fulfillment.

Simply said, SEMS would take profile information directly from SEIS and would use online testing of specific aspects of each applicant profile to match for best possible fit with the requirements of all available job opportunities.

The potential for creating and matching jobs with job applicants would go ***beyond enormous on a global scale***, so there would always be at least two priority considerations to respond to when considering expansion to a global effort.

SANE and ShareFlow would need to use expert talent when designing and setting up the programing applications used to accomplish this task because it would be the very foundation upon which all aspects of the SANE Economy would depend upon.

***The First priority would be to make software and hardware applications foolproof through failsafe testing of all functions prior to going live on the Network.***

It would also need to allow easy and adjustable changes when necessary to evolving conditions in the economy on a local scale as it expands and trends to an eventual global database.

# 5 Employment Matching

***The Second priority would be to plan for an eventual global operation by logical and mathematical testing using typically large numbers that use a hypothetical prototype operation of that magnitude.***

The prototype must be engineered to confirm worthiness of all operations before it is qualified for launch so that it could expand within the Network as more and more Local Banks join the international community and the online operations.

Since the SANE economic model is based upon Local Bank Control based within each Local District in the Network, there would be no practical reason why the offices that manage the matching process could not also be physically located within the Local Banks in a similar manner as the SEIS offices.

This could hold true for the startup and early evolvement of coordination protocol with all subsystems working together to prove credibility and popularity with the public at large.

But once the ***ShareFlow Network evolves sufficiently, a simple transition to alternate buildings and additional locations*** for required logistical convenience would become the order-of-the-day to make for the entire Network operations.

This kind of planning is necessary and should work well when using a cooperative of online internet services and servers interconnected for all necessary communication requirements.

Considering a typical Local Bank set up, it could be called a ***Local Employer Matching Office (LEMO)*** as part of the evolving Network operations.

Responsibilities of each LEMO would be to accept and use individual profile data online from all employers, local and otherwise seeking to fill job openings in their specific Local Bank District

All employer information within LEMO would be stored within a ***Master Employer Database (MED)*** for processing to enable the first part of the matchup operations as close to real time as possible.

A second database could be called the ***Master Applicant Database (MAD)*** containing separate profile data submitted online from all employment applicants within the District.

# 5 Employment Matching

***MAD*** profiles would be used in conjunction with ***MED*** profiles as the necessary second part of the matching process.

Once data from all profiles presently available from both sources is established, each matching office (SEMS) would begin comparison matching to locate the best possible matches of mutually suitable jobs and qualified personnel to fill all available job openings.

**With respect to the Employer Data Profiles MED, the first consideration would be to code each employer's specific job offer, and have it tagged for processing with respect to all job types offered by each employer,**

Another consideration could include the specific locations of each position presently open in real time so that this aspect for matching is identified and coded for comparison with all ***Job Applicant Data Profiles in MAD.***

A third consideration could logically be a filtering process targeting the ***salary levels*** then being offered for each specific job opening to be coded for processing.

Next might be the various specifics of ***desirable and required experience*** inclusions that need to be considered for each specific job opening that is available in real time.

Another important factor of any job opening would be desirable windows capped at ***upper and lower age limits normally preferred*** for each job opening.

Along with age preferences, all prospective Employee health considerations would be a factor in many job types and need to be considered and coded for the matching process to help find the best matchups for all job openings.

***Desirable educational levels*** would be one of the most important consideration for most job offers, but ***in many cases would not have to be a limiting factor.***

Another important variable for any job opening would be looking ***at issues of security, character and attitude*** that could affect performance as well as safety for employees.

However not all jobs would necessarily need all these aspects factored in specifically, depending upon security issues for the company and other employees.

# 5 Employment Matching

A few jobs have hazardous duty issues that need to be flagged if necessary so that all job applicants are matched accordingly to their preferences, concerns and windows of acceptability if deemed significant.

From all prospective employers' points of view, a schedule of desired and necessary work hours per week need to be stated for each opening.

**As a matter of practicality, no disqualification code would need to be used regarding full or part time work necessary for hiring**, however each employer could state their **operations and schedule** preferences for consideration as part of the equation for hiring.

Another consideration for each employer would be to state whether some or all hours of work can be done at home (such as with home-based computer applications, or whether it must be performed partly or wholly at the company offices at the work location environment.

Any other company requirements or preferences should be noted so that the matching process becomes a matter of fine-tuning and filtering to precisely identify the best considerations for hiring new job applicants in each employment situation.

All company offered benefits should be clearly noted on each profile for easy reference by an applicant, and for easy coding in the matching process.

**The second part of the employment matching process would be the profile data submitted by each job applicant ultimately becoming part of the Master Applicant Database MAD** for comparison with all jobs available in the Master Employer Database MED.

Computer processing could tag all profile data with coding to match preferability, desirability and acceptability.

Input data on MAD profiles would include their **priority preferences** such as preferred locations and salary as well as to what degree location and distance from home would still be acceptable for each job applicant.

Practical windows of acceptability for **Salary Range** for each applicant including information about family, lifestyle,

## 5 Employment Matching

dependents and pets, and any other factors that would affect their acceptability requirement related to minimum income preferability could also be included for consideration in the matching process.

Job history and experience in each pertinent area could be indicated on the applicant profiles for easy on-line filtering to eliminate the hassle of hand-written resume input that so often clutter traditional profiles.

Age and health issues could be indicated with easy online input for coding in the matching process.

This would include any limitations on the part of each applicant to accept certain types of work.

**In a non-invasive manner, certain questions regarding an applicant's world view related to personal philosophy could be included as an optional item** that would be pertinent to some types of work that the applicant would feel either best-suited or not well-suited for a logical match.

As an example, many applicants would know in advance they are not suited for politics, law-enforcement, agriculture or real estate, etc. especially if they have no interest or have strong feelings against involvement in any of those areas.

For notable preference however, some applicants could be highly ecologically minded and would likely do well in any matching of employment related to that philosophy.

The level of education that each applicant has reached will be a major consideration for most professional employment and thus could be coded appropriately by each applicant.

If certain job openings are inherently associated with any type of hazardous duty requirements, that information could also be included on the input to each applicant's profile for easy comparison to job match requirements.

Each job applicant would need to indicate **preferred and accepted number of hours per week of employment** except for home-based work environments.

Once all profiles are completed for the MED and MAD databases, the matching process would begin with reasonably

## 5 Employment Matching

high-speed operations to assure results are output on a timely basis and as close to real time output as possible.

**The theory for matching in an efficient manner would consider all pertinent variables for best results.**

Each comparison of matching results for output to both job applicants and employers would nominally consider many applicants submitted to the MAD database as well as many job openings submitted to the MED database.

A window of acceptability for each opening for applicants could typically be set at scores between 85 and 100% (or some other adjustable level) that filters out a certain percentage of profiles not making a pre-set grade for mutual compatibility.

As a reasonable window for mutual compatibility, if there are many job applicants vying for a specific job, the acceptable score could be defined as 90% or higher.

For jobs with few applicants, perhaps only the top 3 scores would be accepted as matching candidates.

**From a job applicant's point of view, they would like many opportunities to choose from and yet not be so overwhelmed by too many choices that practical selection would be an unnecessary task for employer or applicant.**

In this regard, perhaps each job applicant could be given up to 10 or more job choices if the MED database is extensive and far reaching.

For that situation, each job applicant could narrow the field by researching each one in a timely manner that disallows confusion or a lot of unnecessary work.

Once an applicant contacts the company of choice that he or she wishes a personal interview, ShareFlow could easily pay travel costs if needed for an appearance at the interview.

Alternately, an online interview could be arranged using Skype or something similar so that all arrangements could be set up to allow acceptance or rejection of each matchup.

With the goal of **always having more job openings than applicants**, a successful match and job acceptance will likely occur in each case so that all job applicants would likely find

## 5 Employment Matching

their optimum work environment without significant waiting time for them to show up.

ShareFlow would keep track of all successful job matches to maintain autopay for the appropriate salary level of every Employee working in each Local Bank district.

Ongoing checks would be made to include all qualified companies registered for job matching in each Bank district.

*As new job notices come in and are reported (or created) within the offices of SEIS, corresponding profiles are fed into the MED data base to include the updates for all real time employment matching.*

Since the operation of keeping track of job openings, creating new ones and updating each database for both MED and MAD require full time operations and skills unique to the core requirements of ShareFlow and SANE, priorities will be reviewed to operate efficiently.

*Priority for social needs would direct the focus of jobs and new job applicants to all the appropriate areas where the demand for such work is greatest.*

Once autopay levels are established and Wages are paid out to all Employees appropriately, the real-time functionality of ShareFlow becomes well-defined and totally transparent to all Account holders.

This means that anyone can come in to check operations at any ShareFlow Local Bank to evaluate the process and see just how efficient and successful electronic currency can be.

*Electronic Units called Sharos would take the worry and stress out of traditional world views of the purpose and practical use of how money is supposed to be created.*

Any citizen could come in and learn for themselves just how Sharo units would be allocated and used to the benefit of everyone in a cooperative economy.

*A SANE National or Global Economy would no longer be given labels like socialism, anti-capitalism or communism, etc.* since all operations would be under Local Bank control with no individual, corporation or centralized government overseer involved in the operations.

# 5 Employment Matching

With ShareFlow and SANE, ***all systems and operations would be owned, managed and operated by the Account Holders themselves***, i.e. all Employees drawing ShareFlow Wages and all consumers using a ShareFlow Debit Card for purchases in a world of ***new economics*** where only Sharo Electronic Currency would be needed and used.

As depicted in this presentation, the ***SANE Economy could be called the Nuclear Option for a New Economy.***

***It would be a natural process once a critical mass of participants becomes a reality.***

And once it does, it will be unstoppable and could reduce traditional money to a vanishingly small stress point for every man, woman and child on the face of the planet.

Let's take a serious look at how these ShareFlow Account Holders ***(Defined as Employees for any company working for the Common Good*** in a ***100% non-profit*** world would work to the benefit of all, thereby ***eliminating all taxation, undeserved wealth, and virtually all the physical handling and accounting of money*** as we know it.

# ~6~
# Maintenance of ECU Accounts

The first responsibility of the ShareFlow Banking Network would be to establish secure operations 24/7 for maintaining a supply of bank-created money going out in monthly payments to qualified employees in their Local Bank districts.

***It would put qualified amounts of Wage money directly into Wage/Savings Accounts and maintain user-friendly secure operations with every transaction.***

This could be accomplished by drawing a specified number of electronic currency units out of a ***Master Wage Account*** within each Local Bank in advance of the monthly allocations.

Once it is time for monthly payouts, each customer's Wage money would be transferred to their personal ***Wage/Savings Account*** within the Bank and would stay there until the client draws money out to make a purchase.

The second responsibility would be to manage customers' corresponding ***Purchase/Archive Accounts*** also within their Local Banks representing all money that is spent for purchases via use of their Debit Cards.

This would be done by accepting transaction details for each customer purchase of products or services and sending these amounts directly to the Local Bank's ***Purchase/Archive Accounts*** each time the ShareFlow Account Holder takes on the role of a consumer for purchases at any location.

All businesses that accept Debit Payment would be directly linked to the Local Bank each customer has an Account with through the ShareFlow Network for direct Debit of cost.

As a result, ***all necessary credit clearing processes*** are electronically completed for all transactions with no customer ever going into debt for overspending.

## 6 Maintenance of ECU Accounts

With banking under ShareFlow, there would be no future payment considerations that use the common definition of *credit* since that definition of credit would now be totally obsolete in the ShareFlow System.

The only exceptions to the rule would be in leasing or renting, since leasing would still occur on big ticket items like a home or an expensive vehicle.

The common definition of *debt* would *not apply* either in any case under ShareFlow since *leasing* would be treated as a payment schedule for *time in use* instead of ownership.

This makes perfect sense since it would result in no added fees or interest payments and would always be an *autopay agreement* with their Local Bank once their affordability qualifications have been satisfied.

Result: Employee Wage/Savings Accounts would be debited in whole Sharo ECU amounts for *cost of leasing*, and the corresponding cost in Sharos would be deposited in the Purchase/Archive Accounts for *isolating the spent Sharos* and keeping track of purchase history for analysis of economic trending and marketing analysis.

This setup would need to be a *100% secure operation* and guarantee that no money would leak out of the secure path from Bank to Wage Earner and then back to the Bank for their economic trending analysis.

Holding to this policy throughout the ShareFlow Network would *prevent any money from being transferred* to any other person, business, corporation or government.

As new account holders move into the district where any Local Bank is located, they would be encouraged to open a Wage/Savings Account or make changes to their existing one if already set up in a Local Bank elsewhere.

Akin to setting up a new account, each new customer would be given a *nominal security check* and eventually a pass to visit their new Local Bank to inspect, examine and get questions answered regarding the workings and operations that make ShareFlow money not only possible, but guaranteed secure from fraudulent activity.

# 6 Maintenance of ECU Accounts

They would also be given their **One Share Ownership** of the ***Bank*** itself along with a copy of the ***Constitution of ShareFlow and the SANE Economy*** that could be called **SANECon** along with full ***voting rights*** that would support the concept of ***full transparency*** for all Account holders.

Any others who are considering eventual membership in the ShareFlow Network would not get full transparency to start with due to security considerations but would be given a partial introduction to how transparency and the entire system operates along with the offer to attend an introductory class for information they need prior to membership.

Appropriate tours could be set up for the general public in order to scrutinize operations and familiarize themselves with the fine details they need to know before deciding to join.

In addition to tours as part of the educational agenda, day courses in Banking, Personal Budgeting and SANE Economic Principles via the ShareFlow Network would also be offered.

All of this and more would serve as a logical step towards gaining full confidence that any personal account holder could be part of the ***actual ownership of their Local Bank*** in their District as part of the ShareFlow Network.

As partial owners, they do not have to answer to any centralized government control because each Bank would act like a ***franchise of the Network*** and would be ***independently owned*** but operated as an important part of an expanding global network.

For many young people coming onboard for the first time, they would be introduced to a well-organized ***Savings and Debit Pairing*** for their accounts and would be documented for personal information and given ***necessary online links***.

By completing the process, they receive their personalized Debit Card for use anywhere in the ShareFlow Network.

As a child previously covered by an adult family member already in the system, they would transfer financial support to their own Wage/Savings Account after they are given the necessary education of how ShareFlow would work for them.

# 6 Maintenance of ECU Accounts

Since the foundation of all accounts within the Network would be the Wage/Savings Accounts for each customer within a Bank's local district, each client could have the option of setting up personalized sub-accounts for different purposes.

*This could include a small-funds account such as one for everyday-spending like groceries, etc., an exclusive account for higher priced everyday spending, another account for recurring monthly bill payments, and still another account for big ticket items including vehicle and home ownership, etc.*

All bank customers would be given the opportunity to come in and fill out a request for a *certain number of sub-accounts* or simply fill out the information on line to set them all up automatically.

For this type of account management, additional bank personnel would be needed to oversee the process, so that their Employee Status Level working directly for ShareFlow could reflect specific duties and get paid accordingly.

In like manner, there would be others in each local bank to handle corresponding breakdowns of sub-accounts reflecting *Personal Spending History* so that all Sharos taken out of circulation for research purposes could be managed correctly within the Purchase/Archive Accounts.

All information recorded for each bank customer would be made accessible on a *need-to-know basis* for anyone else in the ShareFlow Network no matter where the Local Banks are located and tapped into via *online information sharing and current accountability technology*.

The creation and handling of all clientele *Debit Cards* would be another function of each Local Bank to reflect current technology that allows each customer owner of a Debit Card to *input convenient code numbers* when and where needed each time a purchase is being made.

A choice of which sub-account of one's Wage/Savings Account is to be accessed would be made on the spot at a cashier location by choosing a number (1 to N) in order to use a certain account Level for Debit Card access.

# 6 Maintenance of ECU Accounts

Current technology for keeping code numbering secure would always be used and managed by specific personal within each Local Bank.

The transfer of money between sub-accounts for any bank customer could be handled in much the same way as ordinary money transfer between savings, checking and other accounts are traditionally handled right now.

Each account holder would have full access and control of how many Sharos are to be transferred into each of these sub-accounts for different purposes.

The difference between using ShareFlow and traditional budgeting is that **all sub-accounts with ShareFlow would be either savings accounts or spending history accounts**, with the Bank clientele controlling all the accounts while the Bank and business connectivity technology places all spent money into their Purchase/Archive accounts according to the type of purchases being made.

Whenever a Bank client (Employee of a business) has a change in their Employee status, a proper way to handle the change in Wage money at the Bank after the change will be an additional functionality of Bank personnel.

However, if an Employee is given a raise or a demotion in pay, the appropriate change is applied for by the company that the Employee is working for.

That change would be verified by proper protocol, and the result would be the change in that Employee's salary effective on their next monthly payday.

Another example for a change in salary and subsequent change in the Employee's status is whenever there is a change of dependents needing monetary support by the working Employee such as the birth of a new dependent or the decease of an older one in the family.

A third example is when an Employee changes jobs or occupation, their appropriate salary level can be adjusted accordingly so that there is no tendency for the ShareFlow Economy to trend towards a recession or an inflation that would ordinarily affect economic efficiency.

# 6 Maintenance of ECU Accounts

If an Employee is disciplined for infractions at their job or for breaking a law, either temporary or permanent salary level would be downgraded to reflect the change.

As always, appropriate bank personnel would be on hand to manage the changes as needed.

Finally, the handling of bank account disputes (although likely an infrequent occurrence) would need to have the proper bank technology, guidelines and personnel available to settle issues to the satisfaction of all those affected by the disputes.

There would likely be a need for special agents working at each Local Bank to handle any disputes in an equitable, fair and just manner along with a few Public Relations employees to satisfy the public with ***full operational disclosure*** in order to generate confidence and faith that the Network really does work for everyone at all Employee status levels.

# ~7~
# Expanding the ShareFlow Network

To expand successfully is to have a goal for an end game firmly in mind with full commitment by all-hands-on-deck.

For the Network, initial success can be demonstrated when all ongoing Local Bank operations are devoted to the creation of non-transferable Sharos while excluding all other forms of money such as centrally controlled government currency.

The next step would be to gradually accommodate and add additional ShareFlow Local Banks to form the basis of what could be the *only banking network in the world that would have the potential to act as a major player for global unity.*

This can be done in two ways.

The first option would be to *build new additional banks or convert existing banks or other buildings* to operate with their essential products and services in an existing community.

The second way would be to simply *expand the inclusion of additional bank customers online from an unlimited variety of participants anywhere in the world.*

As long as they were committed to support SANE and hold ShareFlow Bank Accounts for being paid remotely from a Local Bank District, all participants would be qualified.

Their employment would need to be verified, validated and accepted for participation as contributions to the Common Good so *they could be paid ShareFlow Wages and be issued Debit Cards* to purchase ShareFlow Products and Services online for delivery like Amazon and others do today.

Using the first option would have the ShareFlow Network concept set up as a logically planned expansion taking a gradual approach and beginning with additional districts located near an original Local Bank for easy testing and troubleshooting.

# 7 Expanding the ShareFlow Network

Obviously, it would make good sense to identify potential operational problems and get them fixed before expanding to a much larger scale with the Network.

*Once secure linkage, communication and operational validations are accomplished, the ShareFlow monetary concept could easily be introduced to non-contiguous communities to form national and international online Banking supported by ShareFlow.*

*Once ShareFlow goes international, the logical name for the Network could be referred to as the ShareFlow Banking International* (**SBIN**).

Primary responsibilities of **SBIN** would be to create and link additional Local Banks to operate 24/7 in a spirit of full Network cooperation for securely maintaining all activities required for online operations.

This would cover the needs of either an expanded local community already served by a Local Bank, or all of the Banks physically located in separate communities but linked online for identical operations.

As a Network, all Banks would work in full cooperation with the ShareFlow commitment as defined in **SANECon**, the Constitution set up specifically for the SANE Economy and ShareFlow to work together.

The many advantages of having an International Network become obvious and include the fact that additional customers *aka qualified employees of responsible businesses in their communities* are participating to assure mutual success.

*SBIN would then add an increasing variety of both products and services for inclusion of previously excluded business outside the Network due to the use of traditional money for Wages and credit clearing.*

Should customers decide to work in the overlap mode (*reliance on both currencies with separate debit cards*) but using appropriate bank linkage to honor all credit clearing, *ShareFlow could still operate using Sharo money alone*, since all Local Banks would be set up to guarantee that the Network remains free from mixing outside currencies.

# 7 Expanding the ShareFlow Network

Eventually SANE with ShareFlow could be the Dominant Force all over the world to help phase out the use of traditional money and begin the serious unification process to bring all nations together in full economic cooperation.

As the Network expands, it would likely generate increased customer satisfaction with increased ease of operations and a greater variety of products and services by way of additional resources and an expanding workforce.

By the very nature of ShareFlow structuring, we get an automatic increase in variety and demand for new employment that can be **supported automatically with legally created money in Sharos issued as Wages** by each Local Bank under local customer control with all Districts in the Network.

Since there would most likely be a resulting increase in useful products and services produced by new workers getting their Accounts in the ShareFlow Network, the popularity of using simple transfers of electronic currency would continue to increase and be accepted internationally with **exclusive use for all credit-clearing responsibilities**.

Additional favorability factors would include a tax-free economy, the security of non-transferable currency and the freedom from slavery to an outmoded money relic.

**As the Network gradually grows in numbers of Local Bank locations throughout the world, it could give the entire concept of automatic electronic currency unit operations adequate time to fix any faults or weaknesses that might show up along the way.**

Properly planned from the beginning, the Network would likely eliminate most potential problems, but probably not all of them due to simple growing pains usually associated with any new and monumental change such as this.

Potential inefficiencies could probably be spotted early and worked out as group synergy takes over to increase efficiency.

**Bank clientele and the general public working directly or indirectly with ShareFlow would likely realize that they have a true win-win situation to share with neighbors, family and friends alike.**

# 7 Expanding the ShareFlow Network

ShareFlow Banking could operate with specialized apps set up to do essentially all the work that the average citizen had had to face previously in their personal budgeting.

Account holders would simply have to check online for the breakdown for their primary Accounts, sub-accounts and their spending history.

***Saved within their Purchase/Archive Accounts for review to encourage sensible budgeting, their spending history would be a good indicator for their future potential of affordability.***

There would no longer be any worries of bounced checks or going below zero on any account since ShareFlow would keep track of all limits and prevent overspending by anyone anywhere in the Network.

All Account holders could be given choices as to what level of auto-budgeting would work best for their purposes.

***All sub-account requests could be given and set up at the time of application for opening their primary Account initially, or for separate disbursements later.***

Specialized personnel would be needed at each Local Bank to translate computer application languages for all international Account holders when they use a different native language to communicate their information.

For proposed Network expansion, Bank personnel could be given permission by the Account Shareholders who would vote to authorize expansion for all suggested locations.

Voting for the actual choice of locations might take into consideration any trending of favoritism if harassment from those who lean a certain way would seem to be a potential threat to operations.

Prior to each new community approved by customer vote for expansion, ***public education classes in the affected communities could be set up to better prepare citizens for all the necessary changes required due to abandoning traditional money in favor of ShareFlow ECU Currency.***

Having ShareFlow hire new employees to accomplish the logistics for community expansion would be the natural and

## 7 Expanding the ShareFlow Network

beneficial means of operation during the expansion process, since Sharo ECUs could always be created in the necessary amounts needed for paying adequate Wages to these workers.

New workers tapped for hire in their own community to accomplish expansion of banking could also be assigned to work on new Local Banks in nearby Districts.

**Educating the public to consider joining ShareFlow as new Account Holders could give many a feel for the new system before they commit to it.**

This would create a benefit for many by offering them an incentive and assurance that all will be well to make a transition from traditional money to ShareFlow currency.

New Account Holders could offer a reasonable amount of traditional money including any *investments they already own converted to Sharos for their Wage/Savings Account so that previous net worth is recognized.*

By having invested money converted to Sharos, they will know that invested net worth money remaining unconverted would be useless within the ShareFlow Network since it could not be used in any ShareFlow transactions.

As previous investors, they would need to accept a new occupational reality as a worker in a profession to be assigned Employee Status doing work that nets a valid contribution to the Common Good.

**Once a new ShareFlow District is approved for addition to the Network, SANE would create new job openings to be matched with qualified applicants.**

Employees in nearby Districts could plan preparations for a new Local Bank, new stores for products and services and logistical personnel to deliver whatever is needed to construct the new facilities.

In conjunction with each ShareFlow Network expansion, use of hired workers relying on *wages paid with traditional money* would be needed for bringing in labor and materials not directly available within the existing ShareFlow facilities.

Most startups for new Banks for new Districts in the Network would not have everything they needed initially.

# 7 Expanding the ShareFlow Network

With respect to that consideration, most of the workers involved with new district expansion efforts would probably need to use the ***two forms of money in separate transactions*** both for Wages as well as for Purchases.

New workers in the community with previous Accounts and Debit Cards will allow them to obtain whatever is available through ShareFlow by reason of their Employment Status.

Whatever they need that is not supported by ShareFlow would be purchased using traditional debit cards accessing their money still held in those accounts.

**During the initial expansion processes, a practical choice of new Local Banks would consider locations where plentiful supplies of food, fresh water and clean energy sources are available and readily accessed.**

In these locations, ShareFlow Banking customers assigned as workers to expand the Network could use ShareFlow Wages ***for most of their necessities in food and other basics*** yet still use their traditional money for items not yet supported and covered by the Network.

Locally produced food items, bottled water, electric power from clean energy sources, building materials, special needs and anything else not yet produced by ShareFlow workers could be purchased by traditional money interaction with previous banking when necessary.

Let us look at a example of how a ShareFlow community expansion with would work with dual money accounting:

Project: Establish an add-on to the ShareFlow Network Local Bank communities within a small home town called Greenville of about 2500 population in the Midwest U.S.A.

The town council decides to establish a model community for advancement of a fledgling ShareFlow expansion effort.

Let's say that Greenville is basically an ecologically-minded and typically progressive town that ***has accepted significant financial support from a relatively wealthy benefactor*** who has agreed to offer adequate traditional funding for the start of construction, maintenance and service personnel who are not yet supported by ShareFlow currency in the new District.

# 7 Expanding the ShareFlow Network

Being a small home-town environment, Greenville uses local greenhouse production of food, has ample water supplies and allows only renewable clean energy sources for power needs including complete reliance on local Solar and Wind energy conversion systems.

ShareFlow Supported Facilities would include:
One ShareFlow Local Bank
One General Merchandise Store
One Healthcare Medical Clinic
One School for grades K-12.

The chosen Benefactor will pay initial wages for workers providing the construction and placement of all logistics, personnel and training for the new Bank District.

Once work is completed, all operations will be turned over to ShareFlow, officially to be recognized and operate using only Sharo Electronic Currency.

**All previously non-ShareFlow workers will be offered membership in the new Unit for dispensation of ShareFlow Wages, Debit Cards and processing of purchases as part of the expanding Network.**

Consider several examples of newly hired workers hired by ShareFlow who will be paid in ShareFlow Wages:

Tom is hired by ShareFlow to be a foreman to oversee the construction of the new Local Bank.

Tom's expertise and education has given him extensive experience working with blueprints, where in this case he will specify the physical layout as well as the required office space for the new Bank.

He and his wife Jane and their two children Daniel and Linda have just moved into a house in the community but still bank with money at Greenville's traditional bank for much of their spending needs.

Once his duties with the Greenville Project are completed, he will have the option to return to his previous employment status where he would continue at his previous company or continue with the ShareFlow Local Bank community to offer

## 7 Expanding the ShareFlow Network

him permanent Employee Status paid in ShareFlow ECU money as a qualified Account holder.

Consider a few other examples:

Kevin is an independent contractor with experience in all levels of carpentry work previously assigned to major projects such as new bank buildings.

Kevin is hired by ShareFlow to oversee all the construction work required at a new General Merchandise Store that will ultimately carry only the products and services to be purchased locally in ShareFlow money.

**Kevin's Employee Status is assigned as Carpentry Foreman at the new Store construction site and will oversee all carpentry work required at the new facility.**

Kevin can retain his Independent Contractor title but now it relates to his official Employee Status in the Network having shareholder rights, voting privileges and Wages paid in Sharos.

As another example, Linda is hired by ShareFlow to help construct a local Healthcare Medical Clinic by overseeing the computer support layout planning for logistical supplies and all computer software applications required to integrate with the existing District Medical Office Building.

**Linda's Employee Status is set at being a computer software specialist** to oversee the recording of all expenses to handle credit-clearance costs with the new Local Bank.

Maryanne is hired to help set up new procedures within an existing local school that will be converted to ShareFlow-supported status.

With ShareFlow support, the school system will be able to expand to include classes on how SANE and ShareFlow will work to everyone's advantage in the new Network community.

**Maryanne's Employee Status will be set as Principle of the K-12 school** where she will oversee all educational operations and be paid monthly and automatically by the new ShareFlow Local Bank District.

Once the new District operations are finished, all teachers and support personnel working for the school will also become

# 7 Expanding the ShareFlow Network

new members of the ShareFlow Network and be paid monthly in Sharos as part of the ShareFlow community.

Fortunately for the Greenville community, Bill Burrows has offered to be the Chief Benefactor who wants to help establish the new community to eventually move away from using traditional money.

But during the construction and adjustment stages, Bill knows that some traditional money will be needed for non-ShareFlow supported resources, training and expertise.

Bill's Employment Status will be set as Greenville's official ShareFlow Benefactor and will have a ShareFlow Account and ShareFlow Debit Card that allows him access to all products and services supported by ShareFlow.

All other Employees hired by ShareFlow to participate in the new Local Bank development will be paid adequate Wages in Sharos for purchase of everything that will be available to buy with Sharos during the construction period.

*As new employees and expertise come on-board in the Greenville community, a gradual expansion of new products and services previously purchased only with traditional money will now morph into the new system and become available for purchase with Sharos as the financial transition materializes.*

All other monetary needs will temporarily be supported by Bill, who will simply place sufficient **standard funding** from his own traditional account to an existing Greenville bank and have the existing bank issue separate debit cards to employees working for ShareFlow to use for products or services that the ShareFlow Network does not yet have available to support.

During the ShareFlow phase-in process at Greenville, all citizens of the town will be given the option to remain on traditional money for all their purchases until the entire project is completed, or phase over gradually by working part time for ShareFlow and have a ShareFlow Bank Account for Wages and Purchase access with a ShareFlow Debit Card.

During the ShareFlow expansion in Greenville, citizens will simply keep track of their personal financing and budget

## 7 Expanding the ShareFlow Network

analysis when necessary by using two separate debit cards, a traditional card for traditional money and a special Debit Card with ShareFlow using Sharo currency.

*The other method of expanding the ShareFlow Network would simply be to use online internet-type connections for accepting qualified new Employees into the ShareFlow Network that could purchase products and services online at remote locations.*

ShareFlow would verify Employee Status worthiness for using the Network to support work they perform as legitimate contributions to the Common Good.

New members would then sign a Membership Agreement to uphold all the values and responsibilities of SANE and ShareFlow mandated by the SANECon Constitution.

They would need to qualify either online or in person at a Local Bank for acceptance into the Network and be set up with workable links to become established Employees tied to a specific Local Bank for payment of their Wages.

By using both methods, SANE and the Network could work advantageously to help hasten the *future goal* of having the entire global economy transitioned into a Universal Money System with the SANE Economy directing financial traffic to the benefit of everyone including the previously wealthy elite.

# ~8~
# Customer Ownership of the Banks

To provide for financial security and prevention of disruption in bank services, a cooperative of owners and managers of ShareFlow Local Banks could be established that allows full ownership and control of each Bank to be divided equally between all clientele in their respective Bank Districts.

These are simply the ShareFlow Account holders who have all financial responsibilities established for all local transactions to the exclusion of any centralized control.

To make this work efficiently, each Local Bank would need a Board of Directors who manage operations at the direction of all voting shareholders in that District.

Each Bank District can have annual elections held so that the bank customers can vote online to uphold existing officers or elect new ones to manage their Local Bank for another year.

***Guidelines for acceptable policies would be outlined in SANECon (the Constitution for SANE & ShareFlow) previously defined for all existing Banks in the Network)***

SANECon would allow every customer Account Holder to be automatically enrolled as a shareholder to the effect that they would have equal voting rights with all other Account Holders within their Local Bank District.

This would include voting rights for decisions that are made regarding expansion rights or proposed policy changes that affect the entire Network (however large it may get).

Each Bank would have administrators in charge of online voting procedures and would publish their results to the entire Banking Network so that ***all Members of ShareFlow would experience full transparency rights.***

# 8 Customer Ownership of the Banks

*In most cases, simple local majority rule would decide how voting results are applied to policy changes, because no central authority would exist or allowed to control important decisions.*

ShareFlow would hold to the philosophy that automatically allows *every vote to count for all important decisions.*

This philosophy would help promote the sense that every Account Holder could take pride in their part ownership of a system that works to everyone's advantage.

*It would lay out a future vision that anyone could come in to closely inspect operations so that the SANE Economy and the ShareFlow Network's ultimate destiny to form a Universal Monetary System and Global Network of responsible banking would always be visible.*

Result: All participants and potentially new customers of ShareFlow would likely support the Network with greater enthusiasm compared to what it would likely be under a Central Control like the Federal Government for example.

The only requirements applied to each Account Holder in the Network would be that they act and vote responsibly and never try to act fraudulently in any manner.

*Most would be happy to cooperate fully to protect policies, logistics and infrastructure that houses a revered Local Bank containing the sophisticated applications that work to everyone's benefit equally well.*

It will also be expected of every Bank customer that if any contentions arise within the ranks, disputes will be handled in a common-sense manner by the Board of Directors acting like a court to determine fair resolutions satisfactory to everyone.

If there are security threats to try to sabotage the online operations of ShareFlow in any way, there could be special Agents that could be employed as a Local Security Team to protect each Local Bank's facilities and operations with effective common-sense methods.

The Bank's Board of Directors could also hire special Bank Employees to set up *redundant backup capabilities* so that communications within the entire ShareFlow Network would

## 8 Customer Ownership of the Banks

always be maintained for keeping local operations free from any significant downtime.

This would allow transfer of records in the unlikely event that a Local Bank would be put out of commission by a natural weather or man-made disaster

If that did happen however, all records of Bank clientele would be redundantly sent (in real-time) to all other banks in the ShareFlow Network so that operations in the affected area would be easily restored.

As owners of their Local ShareFlow Bank, each Account holder might be ***encouraged but not required*** to take part in community involvement projects that enhance and strengthen the effectiveness of ShareFlow Banking in their area.

Specifically, bank customers could notify their Board of Directors of their awareness concerning a new business such as a new product or service that would be available soon in the District to be included for support in the ShareFlow Network.

As an example, let's say that Michael and Joan who are existing residents of the ShareFlow community of Greenville learn that a new specialty restaurant owned by Larry and Irma plans to relocate to Greenville and will need to purchase some property to build their restaurant at a desired location.

Michael notifies their Bank officials about Larry and Irma's desire to bring in the new restaurant that will need support and workers to build the new facility.

Responding to Michael and Joan, the Local Bank officials arrange for residency and employment for Larry and Irma, and additional workers to construct and set up the business.

By doing so, it would help complement the community's products, service and employment with the addition of one new business due to Michael and Joan's initiative.

**Any Account Holder of the Bank could send out a notice online to any business to encourage relocation to the District as part of ShareFlow's efforts for Network growth and benefit to their community.**

As another example, let's say that Harry and Lisa have pet dogs and cats and realize they need to encourage a veterinary

## 8 Customer Ownership of the Banks

clinic relocation to Greenville to accommodate service to all pets and their owners in the area.

Using standard money to pay for advertising, Harry and Lisa send out their Help Wanted notice for Veterinary Service in Greenville and get a response from an interested Vet Clinic in an out-of-state community.

The result: ShareFlow is notified of the intent of the Vet Service to possibly relocate and become part of the ShareFlow Network of supported companies.

**If ShareFlow would support their efforts, they would bring in a franchise of their business to be included as a pilot facility for complete veterinary services.**

This addition to the Network would add to the totality of products and services offered in Greenville, and all because an existing ShareFlow Bank customer had the desire and initiative to help bring into the community a much-needed service for the growing demand for affordable pet healthcare.

ShareFlow Account holders could also use their initiative at websites to suggest a fine-tuning of Employee Wages either up or down for a specific Employee Status level or simply a fine-tuning of a specific individual's Wage Status due to that person's track record on their job.

**Managers of businesses can always inform ShareFlow of recommended changes of salary for worthy employees who are doing outstanding work and deserve reasonable raises in Wages within their job status level.**

Alternately, that same manager will have the responsibility of reporting substandard work when it is reasonably applicable to do so regarding any Employee if deemed necessary.

**If a worker in the Network needs to be demoted in salary, this could be done as a temporary limitation to allow the Employee time to correct the situation.**

In any case, it would be done commensurate with the severity of infractions or apparent harm to others as a result.

The idea is not to strike out in a punitive manner, but rather to help that person commit to coming back to standard level

## 8 Customer Ownership of the Banks

performance by backing it up with action to improve their track record in whatever area that needs improvement.

For setting prices on products and services, any Account Holder could give recommendations for fine-tuning of the established costs if their suggestion is logical and seen as a benefit to the Common Good.

***The purpose would be to maintain a balance of customer satisfaction levels between businesses and their customers in line with common sense guidelines.***

They can also put in suggestions for a new hire when that person's intentions are known and want to join ShareFlow.

Any non-members of the ShareFlow Network hired for a business that is supported by ShareFlow in their community can simply go to their Local Bank or online to the appropriate website to apply for their Wage/Savings Account and thereby become officially a part of the ShareFlow Family.

***Any Account Holder within a Local Bank District would have the right to vote yea or nay online for a Board of Director's proposal for a new Banking Facility within their ShareFlow District.***

It would be treated like adding a franchise to a local District already supported by at least one other Local Bank.

Another consideration that ShareFlow Account Holders might want to consider would be to report any extensive travel plans they are considering for being outside their District for an extended length of time.

The purpose would be to facilitate a smooth transition of Wage allocation and Product/Service history from their home Bank to an outside Local Bank so that the two Local Banks can adjust to the temporary changes.

These customers could also report temporary reliance on standard money during their travel time, and that they will be using alternate debit cards, one for standard money purchases, and the other for ShareFlow Debit purchases via the Local Bank within the District whenever possible.

Endless examples can be given to where existing Account Holders at a local Bank can contribute to the growth of the

# 8 Customer Ownership of the Banks

Network as well as overall community growth supported by ShareFlow with timely suggestions to help ShareFlow expand in all directions.

Single-Vote Part Ownership of a Local ShareFlow Bank would give each Account Holder a sense of pride in their community by reason of their Employment, their Purchases of products and services, voting rights and new opportunities to participate via suggestions for growth and improvements to help unify their neighborhood and community.

**_Everyone will eventually learn about the New Kid in Town because they will realize that SANE and ShareFlow working together will be the very core and driving force behind a True New World Evolution that will work for the benefit of all and not just the wealthy elite._**

And what about *Universal Electronic Currency* being used for All Wage Payments and Credit-Clearing Purposes?

**_Could a Universal Monetary System prove to be the trigger to bringing an entire global economy to a full roll-over using Cooperation instead of Competition to create an unstoppable that would ultimately benefit everyone?_**

What if ShareFlow became the only viable alternative to business as usual, while simultaneously offering sustainable and healthy living for every man, woman and child on the face of the planet?

## ~9~
## Transparency of Operations

ShareFlow operations will be designed for transparency & education offered to the public to expand the Network and retain public confidence in a spirit of integrity and security in using an alternative currency standard.

Using electronic money, ShareFlow would closely follow guidelines in the SANE & ShareFlow Constitution SANECon by each Local Bank in the ShareFlow Network.

By doing so, each Bank would have the responsibility of maintaining security & dependability 24/7 for all customers.

All Local Banks would be set up to demonstrate to anyone that it could and would maintain fair & secure Wage allocations for all Employed workers in each Bank District.

By doing so, it could remain as the basis of a potentially global encompassing Universal Monetary System for all credit clearing purposes and maintain full transparency in electing the Board of Directors for each Local Bank District.

*Beginning with a minimum of only one Local Bank to set up the entire process as a prototype of operations, ShareFlow could demonstrate full integrity and maintain the basis for unlimited growth.*

Using the Internet or a similar alternative to the existing System, ShareFlow personnel would have the responsibility of balancing bank security with visible transparency.

*As such, all clientele in the system could feel assured that their money is not only safely stored as electronic currency, but that all Local Banks would synchronize to maintain operations without significant problems.*

An additional requirement would be to prove to the public at large that the **chosen unit** of electronic currency known as the Sharo will retain its fixed value indefinitely and thus the

## 9 Transparency of Operations

Network will never allow an anomalous condition in the New Economy such as a depression, recession or inflation.

To provide full transparency, each Bank would set up an auto-inspection procedure to invite the public and potentially new bank Account holders to attend an open-house or a class for public awareness periodically.

***This open-door policy would offer a full inspection of equipment, hardware and software, and a review of every step in the protocol of operations involving transfer of Sharos to and from Customer Accounts.***

Visible to the public at large would be all related facilities and procedures that are used to operate the entire functions defining the alternative economy called SANE (the Socially Automated Network Economy).

Full visibility would be provided to show that SANE could initially have separate offices within each Local Bank during the beginning phases of startup and expansion to eventually including many more Local Banks in the Network.

These separate and supportive offices would each have a function to manage all SANE subdivisions supported by ShareFlow that would eventually move to alternate buildings after enough Local Banks have joined the Network.

***Physical and logistical growth would always be synchronized to encourage participation of a sufficient number of Account Holders to financially support the creation of add-on Banks and related facilities.***

A priority for public inspection would simply be the Sharo money creation process itself, where bank personnel could demonstrate the hardware and software results directly.

Prospective new Account Holders and the public at large could come as individuals or groups to enter the facilities for inspection and learn why the process of Local Bank creation of money is to be favored over mandatory taxation and Central Control of an entire economic money supply.

By seeing how Sharo electronic currency units are created via sophisticated computer applications, the public can educate

## 9 Transparency of Operations

themselves in the reasons why ShareFlow could be considered the *indisputable wave of the future for any economy*.

Complete transparency demonstrations would show what happens whenever an Account Holder does a transaction to affect a Credit Clearing (purchase of a product or service).

It would also show how the process can *guarantees non-transferability of funds* to keep them residing in the Local Bank via ownership of a legitimate Account that earns Wages and transacts business Purchasing of products and services.

This would show directly how Sharos are taken out of the Account Holder's Wage/Savings Account and transferred into a corresponding Purchase/Archive Account for keeping track of *general trends of spending* in the community.

Adding credibility to the transparency demonstrations would be illustrations of typical Account holders by pseudo names showing the entire process from start to finish for all types of money usage and transfer.

After each public demonstration of the Bank's operations are completed, the Local Bank assistants would want to make sure that the inspection team was fully satisfied and confident that their personal money would be safe, and that the Bank's reliability and future sustainability would be assured.

*As part of the public education presentations, Local Bank officials could set up PR Illustrations in the lobbies to let walk-ins get familiarized with the new "Kid on the Block" and the way the new "Kid" does business.*

Each demonstration could consist of active video displays of typical customer participations showing flowcharts labeling the ShareFlow theory and the way that the SANE Economy would distribute funding *only to where it is earned* by reliable Employee Account holders.

Each demonstration could include explanations about why ShareFlow and SANE are committed to the philosophy of supporting only the workers who contribute to the Common Good in definable terms of their professions and the resulting production of products and services.

# 9 Transparency of Operations

As part of the ongoing process to educate the public, each Local Bank could hold day classes to emphasize **Customer Ownership of their Local Bank**.

The classes could show how the **Account Holders vote online** to elect a trustworthy and reliable Board of Directors operating with honesty and integrity at each Bank.

To emphasize SANE and ShareFlow's **commitment to full transparency**, bank officials could show how security coding can be password-friendly and still guarantee adequate security measures for a fraud-free environment.

In the unlikely event of a complete breakdown or a physical destruction of a local facility due to any cause, man-made or otherwise, bank officials could illustrate how the **ShareFlow redundant record keeping process** guarantees that records would not be lost and always retrievable 24/7.

Another feature of ShareFlow's maintenance of complete transparency would be the fact that ShareFlow currency would be *real money yet virtually invisible and exist only as the electronic currency of numbers in customer Accounts*.

PR work could include confidence-building indication of how the money standard could be tied to the cost of water.

For example, the value of a Sharo could be set as The Value of One Gallon of Drinking Water = 1 Sharo to replace the Gold Standard or any other physical standard of currency.

Since water is more important than gold to keep people alive, it should be valued as such to convince the public that ShareFlow money is viable, sensible and has no need of being created in paper money, checks, cash, coins or investments of any kind since these forms of physical money would now be defacto considered archaic and unnecessary.

As another indicator of "sensible" money, it would be convenient to *use Sharo units without fractions.*

Instead for convenience, the System could allow issue and use of Sharos *only in whole integer amounts to avoid the unnecessary precision* that would no longer be required.

This innovation in policy could become a desirable feature to remind everyone that there's much more to life that could

## 9 Transparency of Operations

be considered part of life's true values instead of chasing after the "dollar" or any portions thereof all the time.

ShareFlow will need to demonstrate a full commitment by showing that no coverup of involvement with foreign nations or political entities are tied in with any ShareFlow or SANE Economics operation.

However, as is true in all financial matters within a civilized society, simple privacy measures of confidentiality in place with traditional accounts and net worth information will remain that way just as they are assumed to be in everyday banking.

To insure a *100% Transparency Policy* for SANE and the ShareFlow Economic Balance between customer privacy and security measures, all policies and procedures would be spelled out for public perusal.

**The Document for this would be available online and developed as the Constitution of The SANE Economy (SANECon) which could only be changed by a majority vote of all Account Holders in the Network.**

Properly set up to start with, *SANECon* would likely be changed very infrequently for minor adjustments needed as the Network takes on a natural growth.

This would allow time for Bank Customers to learn how to participate in the voting process when any change is proposed by elected Board Members.

Changes would probably be mostly procedural in nature anyway and would never adversely affect the overall policies of what SANE and ShareFlow are designed to accomplish.

Content for the *SANECon Constitutional Document* could include clear statements of intent that would affect any minor changes that include separate commitments to the major aspects of secure operation:

A statement of the SANE and ShareFlow Economic Philosophy would be stated in *SANECon* to indicate that all factors affecting the flow of currency will be geared to the basic premise of *Value given for Value received.*

*SANECon* **would identify any** *employment that fails to promote the Common Good* so that it could disallow any

## 9 Transparency of Operations

financial support for transactions or employment that seem to be potentially harmful or be in conflict with the premise of ***Value given for Value received***.

***For ShareFlow operations, SANECon would state all the constraints that would fix policy for the ShareFlow money system as follows:***

* The ***1ˢᵗ Section*** would specify that all money will be dispensed as ShareFlow Electronic Currency created as Sharos that ***return to each Local Bank where it was created***.

* No Sharos will be issued to anyone other than reliably Employed Workers or the disabled who earn them resulting from their documented Employee Status.

* No Sharo Money will be transferred to any other person, business or government entity.

* A Network of Local Banks using Universal Sharo Money could expand only via ***Local Control of each Bank***.

* All workers participating in the ShareFlow Network (worldwide) will be given an Employee Status.

* All Employees will be paid regularly, adequately and automatically on a regular Wage payment schedule.

* All traditional currency will be encouraged to trend into obsolescence by replacement with Sharos in the ShareFlow Network expansion.

* ***No taxes of any kind will ever be required by anyone*** as Account Holders the ShareFlow Network.

* All Products and Services will sell using 100% Non-Profit operations with Sharo Currency via a personal Debit Card issued to all Account Holders at the time of their acceptance into the Network.

* Appropriate Universal Single-Payer Healthcare will be developed by SANE for all Account Holders.

* All Public Education will be free for everyone at any age level involving any curriculum of value to the Common Good.

* ***Specific Sharos in circulation will be used only once and then archived for economic trending research***.

* All Products and Services will be value priced fairly and equitably throughout the Network.

# 9 Transparency of Operations

\* *Only Employment types supporting the Common Good will be qualified for ShareFlow participation.*

\* Everyone in ShareFlow will be encouraged to select a type of work best suited for their interest and skills.

\* 100% Renewable Clean Energy will be used for all ShareFlow and SANE operations and facilities.

\* Everyone having ShareFlow Bank Accounts will be disallowed to acquire any Debt, since as commonly defined it is becomes unnecessary in the ShareFlow Network.

\* Political money, poverty and homelessness will virtually disappear due to the feature of Non-Transferability of funds in all financial transactions.

\* All beneficial enterprises will be given the necessary and proper financial support they will need to prosper.

\* All ShareFlow operations will be 100% **transparent to the public**, with no activities accomplished in secret except normal privacy matters considered confidential to each client.

A *2$^{nd}$ Section* of ***SANECon*** can be included to define the Network's commitment to use only Renewable Clean Energy for sources of energy and power which would include the latest technological advances including reliable Solar and Wind Energy Conversion Systems.

A *3$^{rd}$ Section* of ***SANECon*** can be included to define SANE's commitment to Free Public Education.

It would specify that costs of Public Education will be paid for automatically by financially supporting students, teachers and educational facilities for classwork participation at all levels from Kindergarten on up.

It would include all College classes and beyond for all approved course work that can ultimately lead to jobs and employment opportunities that benefit the Common Good.

A *4$^{th}$ Section* of ***SANECon*** could define & specify the procedures and commitment to keep the pricing of all products and services ***at fair and relatively fixed market values*** with only minor adjustments if necessary.

If needed, small adjustments could be made according to priority changes for supply and demand that will help direct sufficient employment to wherever Trending in the Economy is needed the most.

The *5th Section* could specify Individual Income and Net Worth in Sharos allowed within limits set for Maximum and Minimum Incomes for each job specification in line with contributory value to the Common Good.

A *6th Section* could deal with the SANE Philosophy and Policies specifying how a Universal Comprehensive Insurance Plan could be laid out and maintained.

The *7th Section* could detail how SANE would set up and maintain the **Universal Employment Creation** Process to Identify when and where additional priority jobs need to be created so that the existing work force could be adjusted and directed to each trending location to balance out the need.

An *8th and Final Section* of **SANECon** could specify the Commitment, Responsibilities and Procedures to maintain a continuous **Universal Employment Matching** System that would operate in real time to match qualified workers with the jobs they are best suited to handle.

The only employment types to be included for matching with reliable job applicants would be those positions with a **proven track record of benefiting the Common Good** in one way or another.

Fortunately for the average applicant, most professional and skilled labor management companies that offered adequate benefits and opportunities for advancement would qualify

# ~ 10 ~
# Wage Allocations

The very core and primary purpose of ShareFlow will be to see that appropriate compensation is provided fairly and continuously to all Employed workers who hold a job status that generally provides at least some net contributory value to the Common Good.

Employment types such as bartending, casino operators, tobacco dealers, alcoholic beverage selling, production, storage or distribution, violent sports and drug dealers, etc. would not be supported by ShareFlow money.

Wage payments would be accomplished strictly with Sharo electronic currency created and dispensed in amounts justified and commensurate with each Employee's responsibilities.

***Also considered for setting standard Wage levels would be employer reviews and work track records that typical employees with similar job titles are able to maintain under average work conditions.***

All Wage Allocations would be provided automatically with Sharo money continuously created by each Local Bank in the ShareFlow Network and would be dispensed monthly to each Wage/Savings Account set up in their Local District.

All Account Holders could access their earnings and net worth via an Account Summary and a ShareFlow Bank Debit Card every time they make a purchase of any Product or Service.

The heart of the ShareFlow operations is to ***consistently create money*** in amounts that fulfill the requirements for Wage Allocations for each registered Employee in their Local Bank District that is set to be paid on a regular payment schedule.

***All created money would be in whole integral numbers of Sharo electronic currency units placed in the Local Bank's Master Account in preparation for individual***

## 10 Wage Allocations

*dispensations set up on a typical monthly schedule in every Bank District.*

The beauty of this arrangement is that no ShareFlow Local Bank in the Network would ever need to accept any kind of Tax Money because *taxes would never be needed nor allowed.*

All ShareFlow currency would be created as *whole number amounts* in the banks' Master Account to transfer later to each individual Employee Wage/Savings Account within the District.

*For every purchase made by an Account Holder, that cost is auto-transferred from their Wage/Savings Account, deactivated and then placed in their Purchase/Archive Account to keep track of their spending and budget history for later review.*

No money (Sharo Units or otherwise) could ever be transferred *into or out of any Account Holder's ShareFlow Transaction Accounts* and sent to any other Account or entity inside or outside the ShareFlow Network.

A separate office within each Local Bank would assign the actual amounts of *Wage money in Sharos* to be allocated to All Account Holders based upon their Employee Status.

This core requirement would *disallow Wage allocations to be dependent upon profits* from any corporation or company the workers are employed at, since all business and government operations would be *100% Non-Profit.*

Actual dispensation of Wages would be set up to transpire on a regular monthly schedule just like electronic transfers of Social Security, Pension or Investment Companies are done.

Wage money will vary similarly to what normally occurs in traditional employment activities, however once an *Employee's contributory value in useful work is approximated*, regular salaries would be set based upon their *Status of Employment.*

Wages would *not be directly dependent* on how well the management personally rates their employees.

If employees are reliable, trustworthy and working in a *generally acceptable manner,* that information is used to help set the prescribed Wages at the level at which their official *Employee Status* has been pre-determined.

# 10 Wage Allocations

Adjustments up or down could be made in some situations, but everyone is guaranteed a reasonable window of income adjustment if they remain a trusted Employee capable of doing their duties as expected.

The Theory of Wage Allocations within ShareFlow should take all important factors and considerations into account and **not be based upon subjective judgments** that could be used against an Employee if personality clashes occur.

An important consideration would be for managements to **rate job and professional expertise values for every average and normally recognized job situation,** and thus approximate Salaries divided into Tiers with those of lowest contributory value paid the least, and those of highest value paid the most.

Using this type of reasoning, we can select a total of 10 **Contributory Value Tier Levels** for Wage Allocations to be considered as basic standards to cover virtually all types of work and professional job assignments supported by ShareFlow.

A convenient TIER Wage Level Range Assignment might go something like this:

**Tier 1** > Range from 0 to 1000 Sharos/month
**Tier 2** > Range from 1001 to 2000 Sharos/month
**Tier 3** > Range from 2001 to 3000 Sharos/month
**Tier 4** > Range from 3001 to 4000 Sharos/month
**Tier 5** > Range from 4001 to 5000 Sharos/month
**Tier 6** > Range from 5001 to 6000 Sharos/month
**Tier 7** > Range from 6001 to 7000 Sharos/month
**Tier 8** > Range from 7001 to 8000 Sharos/month
**Tier 9** > Range from 8001 to 9000 Sharos/month
**Tier 10** > Range from 9001 to 10000 Sharos/month

By design, this would put a cap on the highest Wages supported by ShareFlow at about **120,000 Sharos per year,** which seems reasonable, considering the logic that **no man, woman or child on the planet needs more than a certain amount of income to attain the highest quality of life reasonably attainable** from the financial aspect point of view.

With this or any similar assignment, ShareFlow could treat each **Tier** as a window of variance to give **employers sufficient**

# 10 Wage Allocations

*latitude in assigning specific Wage Values* within the range of each **Tier** for any job positions defined by an Employer's work requirements.

Also considered would be specialty work types for the more uncommon job classifications to cover other variables deemed important as ShareFlow progresses and expands into a Network with more accurate data available.

To be clear, no matter what **Tier** a worker finds themselves in resulting from their assigned Employment Status, *ShareFlow would make No Class Distinction on any variable for the basis of Wage level or Tier assignment, since everyone will always have ample opportunities* no matter what subjective judgments exist *to advance themselves to a higher Tier level.*

Ample opportunities would be guaranteed through helpful programs that focus on increased education, job experience, health improvement and initial selection from alternate choices of professional expertise, etc.

Consider the *Wage Tier Levels* as follows:

**Tier 1** could be the lowest Level of Wage Allocations that could be defined for those who (for whatever reason) cannot or are unwilling to work in a contributory type of employment.

Everyone at the **Tier 1** Level would receive Sustenance Essentials including food, clothing, housing and basic healthcare; and therefore, could purchase only products and services of that nature at little or no charge.)

**Tier 1** would cover base income for all those who do not or could not contribute directly to the Common Good with useful work including the homeless and disabled and thus are not part of the active workforce but still need to be supported.

A theoretical assignment of Wages for **Tier 1** would include everyone who has a Local Bank Account with Zero to 1000 Sharos/month assigned to their Account payment schedule.

If currently having little or no money coming in, their Debit Cards would be coded so that they could still use it to receive all their qualified sustenance basics free of charge.

To be fair, these free-of-charge essentials at **Tier 1** would also be free of charge to all other Employees as well.

No matter what other level (**Tiers 2-10**) everyone else is assigned to regarding the purchase of necessary products and services beyond the Sustenance Level, every Account Holder would also have access to qualified free basics as part of their quality-of-life choices and ability to maintain.

**Tier 1** Debit Cards would allow Card Holders to select from specified items designated as Free of Charge, but if their personal circumstances change to allow for an up-grade in Employment status, their Cards would be coded for the higher **Tier** Level.

*Wages for Tier 1 > 0 to 1000 Sharos/month.*

**Tier 2** could be for typically low contributory value types of employment, but still be considered work that contributes to the Common Good.

**Tier 2** Wage allocations would apply to those with jobs that have *traditionally had minimum Wage caps* and may have had to scrape to earn a living.

An important difference between ShareFlow and virtually all other banking is that with ShareFlow, all minimum wage type of work would be given **adequate Wages that are not dependent on employer *profit*,** but still limited to give each of them a step above sustenance commodities that do not include luxury item affordability they are not employment-worthy of.

In other words, **Tier 2** could allow a good standard of living but would not support purchases of products or services that tend to exceed values that the Employee's chosen job status would normally contribute to the Common Good.

**Tier 2** would likely cover all the menial task labor jobs that traditionally have not required significant skills or an education beyond elementary school such as farm labor, grounds keeping, simple janitorial work, etc.

**Tier 2** Wages, being auto-paid would be assigned to all Workers whose Wage level might be set but adjustable to anywhere between 1001 and 2000 Sharos per month according to their job expertise as an example.

**Tier 2** Debit Cards would allow the recipients to select from all products and services that were previously designated as Free-of-Charge at the **Tier 1** level for *inclusion* with all other products and services they could afford to pay for at **Tier 2**.

*Wages for Tier 2 > 1001 to 2000 Sharos/month.*

**Tier 3** would define the next level of Wage allocation for all workers that might normally hold jobs and professions that require at least high school education, but generally not much additional formal classwork.

It would allow for somewhat greater responsibilities and for work assignments in professions beyond those included in the previous Wage level.

Employment in professions requiring more skill or more difficult labor-intensive work might include basic assigned task work such as road repair, product quality control, guard duty, nursing assistant work, first level farm labor foreman, etc.

*Wages for Tier 3 > 2001 to 3000 Sharos/month.*

**Tier 4** employment levels might typically include jobs and professional employment that would require two or more years of college, trade school, or on-the job training expertise such as an elementary school teacher, a staff manager, a supervisor or a department head at a general merchandise store, etc.

*Wages for Tier 4 > 3001 to 4000 Sharos/month.*

**Tier 5** employment levels might include all professional employment that requires a college degree in a special field of expertise, four or more years in a trade school, or three or more years of specialized on-the-job training such as with high school teachers, specialty trainers, physician's assistants, or general managers at merchandise stores, etc.

*Wages for Tier 5 > 4001 to 5000 Sharos/month.*

**Tier 6** levels of employment could include professional expertise in a specialized field such as engineering, science or medicine, or having earned a master's degree in education.

Or it could require four years in a trade school plus two or more years of training as a computer programmer, a mechanical engineer, an electrical engineer, a college faculty member or a senior manager at a merchandise store plus others that have had special training to assist in their employment rating.

*Wages for Tier 6 > 5001 to 6000 Sharos/month.*

**Tier 7** logic could include those who responsibly hold public office in government who prove they are contributors in politics or could include those presently in **Tier 6** with a sufficiently long track record of success in their present employment plus those who present other evidence for an upgrade to this level.

*Wages for Tier 7 > 6001 to 7000 Sharos/month.*

**Tier 8** employment levels might include management and professional expertise with extensive experience or have a greater responsibility or specialization such as in engineering or have a PHD degree plus two or more years of on-the-job training.

This might include electrical engineering, civil engineering, computer hardware or software engineering, a college faculty member or have extensive experience as a senior manager for a chain of general merchandise stores, etc.

*Wages for Tier 8 > 7001 to 8000 Sharos/month.*

**Tier 9** pay levels could include CEO level management or professional research and laboratory work expertise in fields such as medical science, space science, astronautics, civil engineering, mathematics, chemistry, etc. plus a PHD in their field, or four or more years of on-the job training plus extensive knowledge in computer science hardware or software, etc.

*Wages for Tier 9 > 8001 to 9000 Sharos/month.*

**Tier 10** employment level could logically include hazardous duty jobs including some levels of dangerous police work or have professional employment that started at **Tier 9** but would qualify for higher Wages due to exceptional experience and track record.

Anything that justified extensive education or training in a type of work that logically should be at a high level of Wages that are ***not dependent on company profit*** but show a measure of true worth and value for public recognition of performance in the Employee's field of expertise could be included at **Tier 10**.

*Wages for Tier 10> 9001 to 10000 Sharos/month.*

When considering Wage allocations, the natural question of how Wages could be managed in a 100% secure and accurate manner would need to be addressed to the satisfaction of each Local Bank's clientele, and preferably to the public and anyone considering membership in the Network.

# 10 Wage Allocations

For them, a brief overview of what takes place to accomplish these tasks could be presented with software applications and illustrations that show simple but important Bank operations performed on schedule without fail.

The overview information would include adequate security checks for each Account Holder and all others wishing to open an Account in their Local Bank.

It could include a presentation about how security-code indicators along with dates and times for each Account Holder's monthly dispensation will occur in their Wage/Savings Account.

An appropriate ShareFlow application would specify the assigned Wage amount to be transferred monthly to each Local Bank Account for easy verification by the Account Holders using their home computers or smart-phones online.

# ~11~
# Debit for Products & Services

*Since all Wage earners are also consumers of products and services they know are needed for living, good health and fulfillment, the use of a simple Debit Card to access their Wage/Savings Account at their Local Bank could be used for everything supported by ShareFlow.*

For every purchase of any Product or Service in the ShareFlow Economic Network, each worker would present their Debit Card to the provider who would simply forward the transaction information (Identification & Debit Amount) to the Local Bank where the Account is held.

All transaction information would go directly to the Bank without any business needing any further action, since *their employees would also be paid directly by ShareFlow.*

Businesses would no longer have a need for a business account since they would all be operating at **100% Non-Profit** and *would no longer require traditional accounts for any direct payments to themselves.*

*All product and service production and distribution to any business would be satisfied by requests for renewal of all necessary commodities from their providers.*

Any request such as these would not need the recipient business paying for the products or services because the workers who fulfill the requests would *also be paid directly by their Local Banks* without need of reimbursement from the businesses they serve.

This allows *a continuity of 100% Non-Profit operations to produce and deliver any Product or Service to any business supported by the Network as well as for Zero Taxes or requirements of any kind for any purchase of anything by any ShareFlow business or consumer.*

# 11 Debit for Products & Services

This my friends would be *Economics pure and simple* and logical enough for even the hard-core legalese of the economic know-it-alls in the present culture of the wealthy who control most of our money to pause and take a serious look at *a more sensible way* for economics to operate.

*Simplicity and Fairness in the availability and use of money is what SANE and ShareFlow are all about.*

Does anyone wonder what else could be easier than having Local Banks creating all the money necessary in the Economy and putting it into circulation only as needed by transferring it from one secure account to another?

Every sensible economist needs to take a serious look at what this *audacious arrangement* can potentially mean for every man, woman and child on the face of the planet.

The only things stopping it right now are the money-controlled politicians and the world of fear and confusion they induce to create the perennial financial crises that run amok to take money out of the hands of those who rightfully deserve and need it to put into the hands of those who don't.

*Assume you are a ShareFlow Account Holder being paid Wages in Sharos.*

You are also a reliable and trustworthy Employee of a business doing all that is expected of you at Company A and wish to purchase your weekly groceries at Store B.

In the simplest terms, you enter Store B, load up your cart, go to the check-stand and run your Debit Card through a Card Reader set up by ShareFlow in a similar manner to what most of us do with ordinary debit cards and traditional accounts.

But instead of paying the cost of your merchandise to a business account at Store B, the online transaction links to your *ShareFlow Local Bank* where your Wage/Savings Account is debited the cost of your purchases.

At the same time, your Purchase Archive Account at your Bank is *updated by that same amount in Sharos* to be archived for future research in local economic trends.

But how does Store B benefit from this?

## 11 Debit for Products & Services

Simply said, all their employees would get paid directly and automatically by ShareFlow Wage dispensations so that they can go on performing their normal work without worry about their job or Wages paid by the store.

***The important lesson for all of us to learn is that the SANE Economy operating with ShareFlow would simply disallow profit for advantage by anyone in the Network, since profit could no longer exist or be necessary.***

With all operations performed in this manner, all necessary work gets completed and likely so in a more efficient way than by a profit-centered system of operation.

Another example >

***Assume you need to purchase a new car at a dealer supported by ShareFlow***, but wait…, think about it!

What you really need is ongoing use of that car, so why pay any budget-busting ownership costs when you can affordably lease and see all repair costs taken care of automatically in your lease agreement?

In the world of SANE Economics, ***leasing would be a viable option for most any big-ticket item*** and would define a sensible ***time-of-ownership*** when the owners commit to pay only for simple maintenance costs to close the deal.

With leasing a car for example, there would be no problem to the car dealer, the buyer or anyone else in the equation.

You could pick out the car you want, hand over your ShareFlow Debit Card and sign a simple Lease Agreement.

Result: You drive away with your new car and have your agreement with ShareFlow that your Wage/Savings Account will be Debited monthly for the simple cost of leasing.

What's in it for the car dealer?

A whole lot, since car sales personnel would no longer finagle for a wheel and deal sale ***but would simply do their job responsibly as Employees by showing all customers and potential buyers their options.***

Sales personnel at the dealership would simply show a prospective customer all they need to know about what they will be paying for to make a wise choice.

# 11 Debit for Products & Services

All *sales personnel at any car dealership* would have all their personal Wages auto-paid by the ShareFlow Network in their community and would have the incentive to *do good work without depending on profit for commissions*.

Result: No matter what business you choose to work for in the sale of a product or service, you as an Employee Account Holder would get paid monthly, automatically, reliably and adequately by the ShareFlow Banking Network.

When you need to purchase the services of a provider where no product is involved, that provider would also be set up as an Employee with a status of Service Provider.

A simple example of a Service Purchase supported by ShareFlow, would be having a piano teacher who is also an Account Holder come to your home to teach you, your child or another adult by ear and be paid regularly by their Local Bank with ShareFlow.

The teacher would have an electronic accounting device to connect your Debit Card to ShareFlow to subtract the cost of your piano lessons with a transfer from *your Wage/Savings Account to your Purchase/Archive Account* that already exists within your Local Bank.

*The teacher would be auto-paid as a self-employed worker with an Employee status of Music Teacher* who holds that distinction if he or she continues to maintain a track record of success within the community.

*Suppose you wish to purchase a new home.*

Let us see how the financial arrangement would work *with ShareFlow Banking*.

Let us assume that the usual purchase of a home no matter what price level we are talking about is handled *either as a direct purchase for ownership or as a lease agreement* in the same manner as many home buyers do nowadays for as long as the buyer and family occupy their leased home.

*A direct purchase for home ownership* would simply be allowed only for those who already have the funds in their Wage/Savings account to be debited as a lump sum or monthly payments to pay for their ownership and give evidence that

## 11 Debit for Products & Services

they are responsible enough to continue their occupation and maintain their status of affordability.

They would need to show that they are an *Employee of a business that contributes enough to the Common Good to afford to pay for and qualify for direct purchase.*

A simple Debit Card transaction and automatic monthly Mortgage payment agreement would complete the deal with no interest or taxes involved, and the new homeowner is given the keys of ownership with no further complications.

*For those who wish to lease as a rental of their new home (whatever the price), a slightly different type of agreement would need to be signed.*

This is a similar purchase agreement that allows affordable monthly mortgage payments to be debited from the buyer's Wage/Savings Account and taken out automatically so that the new home owner is paying for a *time-of-ownership* leasing instead of a direct purchase.

Whichever type of transaction is chosen, there would be no hidden fees or complications that traditional renting ensues.

In either case, there is *no interest involved, no debt incurred, and the sales personnel need no commissions based upon any profit because profit could not exist.*

Instead they would be paid automatically by their Local Bank in line with *their Employee* **status being responsible Realtors** doing the kind of work they love.

Consider now the purchase of various **Tiers** of *Health Insurance Coverage*, all of which simply treat each Level as a Copay type of arrangement where no additional costs accrue for treatments within the level of selected coverage.

Specifically, let's say that you as an average adult with wife and two children choose **Tier 4** healthcare coverage for your *all-encompassing level of Universal* **Insurance that you and your advisors** decide is adequate for you and your family.

In this example let's say that your monthly Debit Payment is simply 200 Sharos with many basic costs waived at the lowest TIER level already offered to everyone who does not or cannot work for whatever reason.

## 11 Debit for Products & Services

Result: Your monthly Wages of say **3500 Sharos** is debited automatically by **200 Sharos** from your Wage/Savings just like other purchases that are auto-paid to take care of all reasonable medical cost coverage offered at **Tier 4**.

As another example, let's say your Employee Status earns you and your family the same **3500 Sharo** Wages monthly, but you and your wife decide you will need additional coverage for your children that the **Tier 5** level covers.

**Tier 5** would offer everything that **Tier 4** offers plus the additional coverage that you and your family decides might be necessary as your children grow older.

In this case, your auto-paid Wage/Savings Account is debited by **250 Sharos** each month which is still affordable but selected at an acceptable higher cost due to the additional needs to be covered.

In all cases of Health and Medical Insurance coverage, there would be *no additional costs* required of you or your family as long as your treatments are not outside the **Tier** level you have selected as adequate.

All prescription costs *deemed necessary* by you and your doctor would be covered within any **Tier** level you choose as adequate for your family's needs.

However, *any elective costs would be added in a generic manner* to ensure that any traditional pharmaceutical profit abuse would no longer be possible.

*Now consider what happens if a person decides to be a candidate for public office* (at any level) from city council to mayor to state governor to representative to senator or even all the way to the *presidency.*

Whatever the level of office being sought after, that person must submit to a reasonable and sensible nominating process and then be called up for an appropriate public election.

In all cases, the financial arrangements through ShareFlow would assign them their *temporary Employee Status as a Candidate running for Office* which would allow them a temporary supplement to their monthly Wage Payments they were previously earning.

# 11 Debit for Products & Services

All candidates would be held to a strict requirement to use only *qualified equal money* for their respective campaigns.

No other money would be allowed for use as campaign support for any candidates at any level including those running for Governor, Congress, or even the Presidency.

All would hold temporary Employee Status running for office in their campaigns recognized at their qualified level.

*All extra campaign Wages would be adjusted up or down as needed after the elections are over.*

With this arrangement, every politician would be limited to appropriate campaign expenses only, and thus ShareFlow and SANE would strictly disallow any additional money to be used fraudulently and politically against opponents or anyone else running for office in any election at any level.

*Essentially, this would demolish all "Politics" as we know it and have known for generations before us.*

It would help bring all *potentially worthy candidates and office holders* to the forefront and onto a level playing field where their true worth must be displayed instead of allowing their campaigns to keep grasping for more and more money to try to outdo the other candidates.

*Consider now what needs to occur whenever there is a transfer of ownership* between two citizens regarding things like a business, private acreage, a home, a vehicle or an appliance, etc. operating under ShareFlow.

If the transfer involves direct ownership and not leasing, consider Citizen A wishing to sell to Citizen B.

Citizen B uses a *Major Debit Transaction Option* and the entire amount of sale is either taken out of B's Wage/Savings Account in ShareFlow or is set up for auto-pay to A's Wage/Savings Account with reciprocal record tallies in B's Purchase/Archive Account.

Citizen A's Local Bank Account is adjusted to add a net value *increase in the number of Sharos to the Account* at present item value, or a release of auto-pay to A's account if that was the previous arrangement and the Item of Purchase is completely paid for.

## 11 Debit for Products & Services

Citizen B needs to show affordability according to his or her Employee Status Wage level and net worth in the bank account to support the sale.

***B's Account would be adjusted by a decrease in Sharos for the value of the sold item or be set up for an auto-pay to pay monthly for lease*** and use of the sold item until the total value of the lease is paid for.

In all cases of direct sale or lease, adjustments in the bank accounts are made ***appropriately by the ownership value*** for payments being made monthly if auto-pay is the option.

***There would never be any interest or fees involved.***

***There would only be simple monetary transactions reflecting transfer of value from one person to the other and instructions being sent to the appropriate Local Bank to set up auto-pay*** if needed.

Maintaining the strict requirement that no money is ever transferred between citizens directly, all transfer of values between citizens would be done indirectly through exercising software apps that Local Banks could use to verify and record legitimate transactions.

Consider now what would happen if a ***ShareFlow Local Bank Account would be tapped to generate a negative balance*** either accidently or purposely.

The first instance (accidently) would not be allowed since that would signal an event where the basis of ***value given for value received*** was violated due to a fault in the system.

In this case the fault would be detected and disallowed.

In the second case, sufficient checks and balances with all ShareFlow Accounts involved would prevent going below zero because purposeful negative balances would be flagged and simply stopped before it could happen.

In either case, once flagged, such an event would be investigated, and the appropriate action would be applied.

But what about situations where everyone is acting in a ***responsible manner,*** but an Account might try to go ***below zero*** because of ***an inability of Wages*** to keep up with auto-

## 11 Debit for Products & Services

pay debits of an item that becomes unaffordable by the Account Holder after the time it was set up and working?

A prime example would be a homeowner paying for a new home with auto-pay having a set amount taken out of their Wage/Savings Account monthly where debits were well within the range of affordability to start with, but later the homeowner could no longer keep up to make the payment schedule.

A bigger question now presents itself: **What's wrong with allowing a bank account to go into negative territory** if there is a compensating mechanism that avoids the **stigma of debt,** but defines an **allowable and rational adjustment** to use for solving the issue logically?

The answer is: There is nothing wrong with it!

**Since mathematics is the basis of everything that exists and operates quite nicely with negative numbers all the time, why not allow the same reasoning to make things fair and justifiable for everyone concerned?**

ShareFlow could do this as follows:

**ShareFlow could allow a Bank Account to go negative without calling it Debt,** and simply adjust monthly Wage payments downward to reflect the Account Holder's lost affordability while **keeping track of the negative balance.**

One option for an Account Holder then would be to re-budget their expenditures to allow a greater portion of their Wages to catch up for their previous regular auto-pay by some reasonable point in time.

In extreme disconnects of Wages and ability to keep on auto-pay, ShareFlow and the Account Holder could work out some other fair solution for all parties concerned.

Result: While the Bank Account is in negative territory, the Account Holder must temporarily adjust to accept a **slightly lower standard of living** yet not be affected so significantly that they would lose any necessities of life such as their home, their job or their means of transportation, etc.

Simple financial adjustments with ShareFlow could take care of problems like these in a logical straightforward manner and allow a homeowner time to re-budget and either sell and

## 11 Debit for Products & Services

move into a more affordable house, or simply be given time to pay off what *looks like Debt* but is not treated as such.

Whatever arrangements are made, they should be such that he or she would have ample opportunities to keep their home and other necessities until Wage payments could *catch up for the ability to pay* the original or adjusted auto-pay amount.

In a similar manner, any other item that is being auto-paid through ShareFlow could be handled in the same manner so that no undeserving shock is applied to a ShareFlow Account Holder if their *Balance goes temporarily negative*.

Any negative Account Balance could be handled either with a change to Employee Status, spending limits or auto-pay adjustments to gradually raise the Balance back into positive territory without a stigma of Debt or punishing penalty applied to anyone acting in good faith.

For all those who willfully might try to take advantage of a negative Balance capability, ShareFlow could use other means to flag and stop such an attempt by applying a just penalty fee to discourage any further activity of this nature.

Financial crime such as Identity Theft would not exist with ShareFlow, nor could any other money-related crime succeed since appropriate security would be in place to flag it all as outlined in the next Chapter on Financial Accountability.

# ~12~
# Financial Accountability

In any economic model, the basic requirement of financial accountability is called credit-clearing or paying off debt by satisfying obligations universally recognized and accepted.

These responsibilities are defined in both a moral and a legal framework as well as business laws that are set to protect all people involved in financial transactions from harm due to failure of clearing credit-debt successfully.

In our present systems throughout the world, this implies **payment of all taxes and keeping all business and personal accounts positive by never allowing any attempt to go below zero go unpunished** after an acceptable "grace-period" has been tried and failed to elicit payments.

The other side of this non-consumer-friendly picture is the aspect of **government control of the money** and a convenient loss of memory that they (**the money controllers) are also expected to credit-clear their accounts** even when they think they are not morally obligated to do so.

Politically speaking, credit-clearing is **not always upheld in business and government transactions** because there is little or no oversight in the hierarchy of control to hold those responsible to their financial expectations.

Having the means to control large sums of money, most governments, corporations and businesses are generally more interested in having their constituents **toe-the-line by legal obligation** instead of moral fortitude.

For them, payment of all taxes and **keeping business and personal bank accounts from going below zero** is forcibly mandated through frequent reminders, harassment, add-on fees or threat of punishment even if extenuating circumstances

## 12 Financial Accountability

*force unaffordability to challenge the rule of man that we must pay our bills or else.*

The important issue here is that in any *sensible economy, monetary accountability is assumed* for all hands-on-deck (the deck referring to the planet on which we reside) and not just to the *99% controlled by the 1% of the controlling wealthy elite.*

Fortunately, **The SANE Economy using a ShareFlow Electronic Currency System is designed to take care of virtually all credit-clearing infractions involving money accountability for any man, woman or child on Earth in many ways once it gets a successful start.**

For any typical consumer, worker and participant in ShareFlow as an Account Holder, secure constraints would be built into the system so that *no income to a Wage/Savings Account could go below a sensible minimum* for any ShareFlow Account Holder.

Likewise, *no income to an Account could go above a maximum cap in any Tier Level of Wage payments* due to constraints put in place and maintained by the Network.

Having these caps on both ends of each Tier window for Income in the spectrum of Wage payments guarantees that all Account Holders are automatically held to payments within sensible restraints that their Employee Status will allow on a reliable and accountable credit-clearing budget-balance basis.

ShareFlow operating within each Local Banking Network would simplify all monetary transactions across the board by eliminating or reducing the scope of any business accounting that has to do with traditional money such as tax preparation or consolidation of debts, etc.

This means that the accepted Definition of Financial Accountability will take on a whole new holistic but simplified focus by *eliminating all unnecessary employment and professions that would no longer contribute to human benefit defined as the Common Good.*

ShareFlow will also free up many types of employment in the "Wish List" of occupations that would lend themselves

## 12 Financial Accountability

closely to those who want to do the work they love without being forced into something just to earn money to survive.

Wherever the ShareFlow Network would extend, Account Holders would be able to *live life in a more satisfying manner* by redefining *quality of life* in terms of peace, good health, joy and satisfaction of doing the work they love.

They could do so without having the burden of stress, desperation or worry over having to work at something or "anything" just to pay their bills and survive.

Thus, the meaning of *financial accountability* could take on a *much more user-friendly quality* that most anyone in the global environment could quickly learn to appreciate.

ShareFlow could virtually eliminate financial fraud of all types by the nature of how money is transacted.

Security could include adequate procedures on how reliable electronic currency is created and how Wages would be allocated only to those who earn it in proper amounts.

Account Holders would know that funds could not be diverted to any other entity's account because of the restraint nature of coded security checks and balances tied to all Wage and credit-clearing transactions.

Keep in mind here that *credit-clearing* with ShareFlow simply refers to the payment of immediate purchase cost either *in full or in interest-free premiums paid monthly* by way of a time-sharing leasing agreement with no loan arrangements ever created, attached or required

Likewise, it implies how Sharo currency would be used for all Wage dispensations and purchase of goods and services that securely disallow fraud and preserve accountability by allowing *transaction electronics to change ECU storage location within each Local Bank* to accomplish these purposes.

Remember > All money that pays for something would be moved from Wage/Savings to a Purchase/Archive Account to provide a *non-transferable* and *transparent history* of all transactions that would auto-stop any attempt at trying to side-step financial accountability.

# 12 Financial Accountability

With ShareFlow in operation, *a new financial reality could emerge* to show evidence that personal attacks of any form to acquire any kind of unearned money as in robbery, burglary, embezzlement, blackmail, extortion, password theft or white-collar crimes at the workplace would be eliminated.

The *age-old crime of counterfeiting would be booted out-of-town with ShareFlow and SANE* since there would be no physical money or way to add fake electronic currency to any Account due to built-in adequate security measures.

Considering things that are legal but not in the best interest of improving the quality of life for anyone such as lotteries, gambling casinos, dog & horse racing or anything involving large transfers of money as we know it today would not be supported by ShareFlow.

Using animals in sports would no longer be tolerated in a ShareFlow and SANE way of living, since traditional money would no longer be involved to accumulate any profit.

With ShareFlow, most wild animals would be protected and respected for trying to establish an improved *quality of life* in an eco-balanced environment.

*Most of the framework of legalities and the language of legalese would be simplified.*

*Ethics would be redefined to include many previously ignored issues that have been traditionally left out of the equation of true quality living.*

*Using ShareFlow, a new world vision will emerge*, leaving citizens the freedom of finding *professions they truly love to put their heart and soul into* instead of resorting to *band-aid income* to temporarily relieve them from the *slavery of forced accountability*.

Considering the punitive nature of our justice systems, ShareFlow would *eliminate the tradition of over-the-top severity of punishments* for anyone who would try to abuse credit-clearing agreements when defaulting for payment of products or services on an agreed-upon payment schedule.

## 12 Financial Accountability

ShareFlow would simply use other ***non-abusive means*** to secure a just outcome if anyone tries to spend beyond their means and consider accountability as a non-priority.

The ShareFlow and SANE ***constitutional commitment of SANECon*** would eliminate the excessive incomes of sports stars, and as a side effect help reduce injuries to players who feel they have to over-reach just to impress their management and fans to earn huge incomes in contracts.

Instead, ***the focus would be on sportsmanship and fair competition*** rather than trying to satisfy the ***flagrant use of money manipulation*** for greater profit and esteem.

More useful side-effects of Locally-Created Currency and control by Account Holders at their Local Banks would be the ***eventual elimination of the Stock Market, the Federal Reserve, the IRS and private investments of all types.***

Why would the locally owned Banks have no need of profit for themselves?

The answer is simple.

It's because each of the Banks' employees (including the Bank Management Team) would be operating ***independently of any need of profit*** since all of them would be adequately paid with ***earned Wages*** put into their personal Wage/Savings Accounts and being unaltered by any other action.

No matter what position they hold at their Local Bank, every Bank Employee would have access only to their own Wage amounts earned via their Employee Work Status.

As Employees working directly for their Local Bank, they could not alter or add to their income by any action taken on their part while on the job or in any other manner.

***ShareFlow would eventually eliminate the need for all financial advisors, tax preparers, the buying & selling of gold, and any other profession of similarity since each of these employment types rely mostly on Making Profit as their excuse for existence.***

Considering the legal world, most legalese and the work involving the management and protection of legal issues would disappear with the advent of the ShareFlow Network.

# 12 Financial Accountability

With SANE and ShareFlow defining a New Economy, all money management & accountability issues disappear before they became a matter of contention.

***If personal property rights are in question***, ShareFlow would address and resolve any issue by simply adjusting either personal Wage/Savings Accounts up or down, or by adjusting the price one must pay to purchase, lease or claim ownership.

All legal decisions would have to be justified in a common-sense manner after every factor is taken into consideration.

***There would never be complex court cases necessary since electronic data verifications would put all pertinent facts together to arrive at fair and just conclusions.***

ShareFlow could significantly reduce the need for having attorneys, but those still needed would be paid automatically, and only with Wages put into their personal Wage/Savings Accounts to be compliant with amounts considered adequate and just for any Account Holder with status as an attorney.

***The future goal of the ShareFlow Network could very likely be defined as the complete elimination of all the imbalances in the business-for-profit culture we have all become slaves to.***

# ~13~
# Government Cooperation

*Any sensible Government should support ShareFlow and The SANE Economy if it takes the step of educating themselves about what SANE's true potential could do.*

When the SANE Economy is finally launched as a start-up network of ShareFlow Banks, the obvious concern to anyone evenly remotely aware of its features is how secure would it be.

Whether the culture of modern economics could change for the better would be based upon the question of: Could a system of this nature operate securely in good faith for all concerned without traditional government interference?

Once the basic safety net of legal non-interference laws is established, is there any government that can take a hard look at business-as-usual fiscal policies and consider the possibility of a ***dramatic change in thinking*** to embrace a new way of doing business to ***work well for all?***

These are open questions with no clear answers, but with the predominantly conservative environment in present politics in the U.S. and in other nations controlling most of the world's money, most folks including myself could credibly give the answer a conclusive No… not at this time.

However, perhaps many others would respond with great excitement and a Yes… once the business-as-usual crowd in politics gets out of the way and lets the people of a nation or culture exert their right of freedom to govern themselves as a sensible cooperative rather than a trending fascist dictatorship.

Presently, any monumental change of attitude on the part of government leaders to ***fully cooperate for commitment to legalized protection*** in the fashioning of a new System of this nature is apparently not forthcoming…unless of course enough momentum of the masses comes their way to demand it.

## 13 Government Cooperation

As a result, any band-aid changes would always leave the way open for harassment including an eventual fascist takeover for a shutdown of sensible choices that would benefit everyone in a workable self-government if it was left to do so.

Fortunately, there are ways to counter any interference or harassment from our government, but it would take *a holistic approach with all weapons of common sense* at our disposal to prevent stone-walling our civil rights to oppose this tyranny.

At this point, the idea of a new holistic structuring for a ***Universal Constitution for Human Rights*** covering all nations as a Union of Common Purpose comes to mind, but of course present day thinking by hard-core conservatives who have a choice to make that happen seems nowhere in sight.

Our first weapon to trend ourselves towards full government cooperation and deflect negate interference or harassment from any source with respect to SANE and the ShareFlow Monetary System is Public Education.

***Well planned Public Education could go a long way to settle the potential fears of conservatives and begin a new trend of thought such that a complete makeover of our Economy is sensibly possible and justifiably necessary.***

Maintaining effective public education could encourage a desirability to demolish the culture of Me-First attitudes that still prevails with many who abuse their legalized money control.

Public education could begin at the local level anywhere and everywhere, and be designed and fashioned for many age levels, potentially for all ages between 12-100).

Appropriate levels of simplicity could be built in for educating young people and be designed as much as possible for simple play-acting demonstrations in their classrooms.

By using the Internet to illustrate the ramifications of a SANE Supported District where a Local Bank is operating exclusively with electronic currency, *effective teaching could reach a wide range of audience internationally*.

Videos could be produced for use in any classroom setting to illustrate what happens when SANE and ShareFlow are allowed free rein to work together to expand exponentially.

# 13 Government Cooperation

Video presentations could show the comparison with what happens when ill-advised laws or ordinances step in and try to shutdown processes that could be very beneficial to humanity.

A two-step approach could be used for demonstration to all appropriate age levels stating the numerous advantages of a ShareFlow System that could easily be seen and understood.

***These demonstrations could reinforce the predicted results with illustrations of what actually goes wrong in many corporations and business as usual economic trends where ShareFlow does not exist.***

Showing what happens when a ShareFlow Local Bank can gradually take hold in local communities would likely give an impressive contrast to the alternatives.

This approach can expand the public educational process to other communities statewide and nationwide to reinforce increased public awareness and the likelihood of sustained growth and popularity with word-of-mouth advertising.

***Public education would help ShareFlow to effectively set up resistance to any political interference or the threat of harassment resulting from ignorance of the system.***

As part of the educational thrust at any age level and specifically for deep thinkers, a provision could be set in the SANE & ShareFlow Constitution **SANECon** that the SANE Economy will be flexible and open to intelligent adjustments whenever slight functionality changes are needed.

Tweaking the Rules of Operation would likely be minimal and applied only if deemed necessary by Account Holder Vote.

It might need to consider technological changes that could tend to compromise functionality if not applied correctly.

Whatever changes decided upon would need to maintain the simple but incontrovertible premise of **value received for value earned** philosophy for every man, woman and child on the face of the planet.

To increase acceptance of the SANE and ShareFlow systems on an international level, the Internet or a modified version of the Internet could be used for translated language copies of all documents as a standard public presentation.

## 13 Government Cooperation

Potential rogue governments who do not allow freedom of information to get to their people will be a greater challenge, but sooner or later truth will flow freely into their awareness that cannot forever be shut off.

*The kind of change we are talking about is inevitable in a changing world of technological breakthroughs and increased demand that people and their quality of life come first before mandated Profit considerations.*

The simple answer for ultimate success of a trending ShareFlow and SANE expansion could only be assured when enough of the national and international populace overcome mindsets, awaken to their true potential, and shake off the corrupt slavery states imposed by their controlling regimes.

*Those who commit to a Global Green Future such as what some independent socially-minded political parties are inclined to do could lend their support with their vote to counter the dysfunctional two-party grip in the U.S.*

In this author's eyes, the **Red's** and the **Blues** have clearly demonstrated a lack of commitment to beneficial social changes so the time is nigh for the **Greens** to assertively step in.

***Status quo supporters*** have clearly shown a breakdown in the ability to respond to the real needs of the people by ***disallowing necessary financial support*** where it is needed the most.

It will soon become obvious to many that ShareFlow and SANE Economic thinking is *not limited to the United States as the defacto location* for an effective startup.

In fact, it could easily start up in more progressive nations that already have social awareness and supportive environments such as in northern Europe, Australia, Canada, etc.

This means that greater time and energy could be put to efficient use for *speeding up international acceptance* using all the tools at hand in a concerted effort to educate the masses.

At this time, there seems to be no logical reason why the **ShareFlow Monetary System using only Non-Transferable Electronic Currency Units** could not begin as an alternative in

# 13 Government Cooperation

countries that are more conducive to social needs given that the spread of the Internet can reach most people all over the world.

Logically it could begin that way once all-hands-on-deck become schooled in the overlying principles of operation.

That being said, it would seem imperative to have an in-house Constitution set up to protect the intent of operation as well as the principles of methodology.

This author suggests that the name for the ShareFlow and SANE Economic Constitution be called SANECon.

Seemingly simple logic would show to all intelligent citizens exactly how the ShareFlow Network could benefit anyone and everyone at any level of net worth in today's global society.

Once the idea is sold adequately to the **first entrepreneur who is willing to build or purchase an existing bank** that would have economic jurisdiction to service a small Bank District, the first concern would be legalities and sufficient guarantees that it must never be allowed to become illegal to operate as planned with SANECon at any future time.

**This would be in the form of a commitment for all governments to abide by the constitutional authority of SANECon so that ShareFlow and SANE could never be shut down currently or at any time in the future.**

To try to stop it would be an obvious affront to the health and welfare of the entire global society, and certainly the very people it was put in place to serve & protect in the first place.

Included in SANECon could be a statement that assumes the highest level of authority to arrest anyone who might try to harass or interfere with the ShareFlow Banking Network.

Logic says that the obvious motive of attempting to stop it would clearly be tied to greed, wealth accumulation and money control, and not be based upon logical reasoning.

Obvious to most, any money in the wrong hands can and does result in great harm to those who deserve fair Wages but are forced to struggle to get it and use it to good advantage.

If that goal seems too difficult, then the answer is to let the people of any nation that favors SANE and ShareFlow fight

## 13 Government Cooperation

for, grow and expand the System to make government or any other type of interference *irrelevant to unstoppable growth*.

*Sufficient growth and expansion in local communities everywhere could eventually override rogue resistance attempted by governments to might try to stone-wall an idea whose time has surely arrived.*

In other words, the idea is too powerful to allow a fascist dictatorship of any type to interfere.

A message to those who might try is: ***You can't win if you're trying to stop The Wave of the Future.***

By popular demand and assertiveness of the people, the energy of social justice could force any abusive ruling class to a state of irrelevancy with respect to attacks or intimidation.

The overriding concern would be whether SANE and the ShareFlow Network could expand naturally without significant interference and remain secure and free to operate without any serious threat arising along the way.

Threats obviously include attempts at hacking by anyone who would be temporarily in competition with the money source (ShareFlow) as it continues *to grow and expand to replace all other economic systems throughout the world.*

These sources are potentially a serious threat if rogue entities want to continue using the standard money systems in defiance of a revolutionary economic model coming onboard to change the way a civilized society operates.

Is it possible that many cynics will rise to their occasion when they first hear about a serious effort to install a threat to their comfortable mindset?

Logic would step in to say that it becomes a threat to their smug existence protected by legalities and traditional money to hear of anything that would disrupt business-as-usual because of inherent resistance to take the time and effort to educate themselves to the real advantages of Change.

Likely places to find them will be on social media and in plain view extolling the politics of mainstream media.

These are the hardcore doubters and haters of any sensible change to the System that invariably would show up to try to

## 13 Government Cooperation

throw cold-water on anything that looks like a threat to their profits or political enclave of their dysfunctional world view.

Using our vote tied to our true values *instead of voting in fear of what the other voters are going to do* is the wise choice in any election because the only real purpose of voting is to *vote for our true values* regardless of what the others do.

Although our personal votes are relatively small tidbits of energy compared to the mass culture of letting media define our thinking, *voting our values* is a step in the right direction.

In fact, as part of the overall education process at any level, it is abundantly clear that voting *only does good if we vote our conscious out of commitment to our true values* and remind others to do the same.

The SANE Economy stands for most everyone's true values whether they consciously realize it or not, because the basis on which it stands is the core of life, liberty and the pursuit of happiness as well as justice for all, no exceptions.

One way or another, we will need to commit to the idea that we must remove the dysfunctional elements of our Society and governments at all levels to effectively make progress for social justice and protection of all life on the planet.

It is our moral duty to protect not only our personal values, but what we clearly observe how the *values of the masses also matter* equally well.

The bottom line of this kind of education is to *remove the threats to sensible change, and make the changes adjust to the real needs of the people* instead of the profit-motive mindsets of corporations and government.

Installing ShareFlow and the SANE Economy for global expansion will be a *giant step forward for humankind* in the maintenance of a peaceful existence without interference from any source be it government based or otherwise.

The question of when a sensible Economy will be able to use the ShareFlow Monetary Methods and be a reality to the world can be approximated by an *analysis of the likelihood of trending towards a specific change as compared to the*

## 13 Government Cooperation

*likelihood of a diversion away from that change* will take as history moves forward to lay out the actual path.

So, the question arises: What are the factors that make up all the trending (T-Factors) weighed against the diversionary (D-Factors) that will come together to spell out a future result?

A scientific and mathematical approach to answering this question takes root when we realize that future events can be assessed by a simple ***Predictor Model*** of the most likely T-Factors working at odds and challenging the D-Factors that forms an equation to approximate how it will likely work out.

For example, certain factors come to mind in favor of a hypothetical Trending Model, while other factors cannot be ignored to challenge Trending and create a Diversion Model.

Currently, the T-Factors seem to predominate since most people are "fed up" with what we already have, and *many people would agree that a cashless society would be a convenient thing to make business more efficient.*

The predominant T-Factor might be *general awareness of inefficiency and the stress of wasted time and energy forced upon us by taxation, profit taking, and greed* induced by our current money systems throughout the world.

Another related T-Factor is *public awareness of many dysfunctionalities that have caused political corruption and breakdown in maintaining the recognized social needs of all citizens aka politics in general*, where the voting process has failed many citizens throughout the world.

A third and powerful T-Factor would be tied to many technological breakthroughs that unavoidably make electronic currency the viable alternative to physical forms of money even without a *direct transition to total Debit Card use only*.

A fourth T-Factor could be the concern over the increase of crime related to monetary vulnerabilities made possible by numerous ways to use transfer of funds conveniently to avoid financial responsibilities in everyday living.

Some Diversionary Factors to consider are as follows:

# 13 Government Cooperation

One major D-Factor is rampant Political Ineptitude and Ignorance in the way our personal representation is chosen in our elected officials of governments at all levels.

A second D-Factor could be *the monumental inertia of the masses who resist even simple changes out of fear* that whatever happens will turn out worse than what they had.

A third D-Factor could be stated as a *Political System loophole* that allows a good decision to become Law, but also allows future politics to come along later to obliterate the good law out of a *need to punish* their enemies.

A fourth D-Factor could be seen as what could happen when the SANE Economy initially gained good traction but inadequate defense against vocal politicians who would pounce upon it for anything they didn't like in *an effort to get rid of the entire package* SANE already delivered for their benefit.

In such a case, these hard-core vocals would want to revert to their quest for profit and taxation money due to their lack of education to the values of what the *Common Good* really represents for the benefit of all.

The higher levels of truth and holistic perspectives are supposed to be the final say on whether *something good moves forward, forced back or allowed to be modified in an acceptable manner.*

Let us set up a simple mathematical equation involving the variables using adjustable coefficients and a Summation of all the T and D Factors to describe a *Probability of ultimate and sustainable success for the ShareFlow Network and the SANE Economy working together with the probability value of P* as follows:

$$T = a_1 T_1 + a_2 T_2 + a_3 T_3 + a_4 T_4 + \ldots A_N T_N$$

$$D = b_1 D_1 + b_2 D_2 + b_3 D_3 + b_4 D_4 + \ldots B_M D_M$$

$$P = T - D$$

# 13 Government Cooperation

**P** stands for the percent probability of success once the ShareFlow Network is launched with only one Local Bank.

**T** is defined as the summation of all **Trending Factors** in Favor of the Success of ShareFlow and the SANE Economy operating with non-transferable money up to and including **N** total identifiable Trending Factors.

**D** stands for the summation of the **Factors of Diversion** that could threaten the success of ShareFlow and the SANE Economy operating with non-transferable money up to and including **M** total identifiable Diversionary factors.

For practicality, the four **T** and **D** factors defined above may be all that are significant in the final analysis, however, by allowing for a possibility of more undetermined factors, these equations leave it as yet to be adjusted as necessary.

The *Probability of Success* will strongly depend upon the willingness to provide adequate education at all levels so that the process of a hard-sell makeover of the present global economy to a (**S**ocially **A**djusted **N**etwork **E**conomy will more likely become a reality in a reasonable length of time.

To be assured of sustainable government cooperation on an International level, the Internet Media using intelligently created packets of educational material will be needed.

Effective education classes at appropriate levels for every major government on Earth may be required to assure that the Constitution of each Nation can be amended to accept any modifications that a *Universal Monetary System* will require for success in every facet of the Global Economy.

# ~14~
# The True Purpose of Money

What is the true purpose and intent of money?

The answer should be obvious but telling it to many of great wealth or just the well-to-do (of any age, time or economic model), you are likely to get the wrong answer.

From math and a scientific perspective, we could write an equation for a purposeful relationship for money as follows:

$$W_U = S_A \times R_A \times E_A$$

$W_U$ stands for useful work accomplished that is directly proportional to $S_A$ (adequate salaries), $R_A$ (adequate resources) and $E_A$ (an adequate number of Employees to accomplish it)

Another perspective is that **Money is the Potential Energy to accomplish Useful Work to benefit the Common Good.**

In my estimation, any perspective about the true purpose of money is relative to the one defining it and likely reflects how money affects their lifestyle and worldview if they have one.

I happen to think that the original intent of the use of money was simply to form an efficient way to assure that the premise of **Value Given for Value Received** is always maintained.

Another side effect to that end was apparently to minimize the use of bartering as a matter of convenience.

With the advent of modern civilization, the ordinary citizen has been forced into a regimen where they must rely more and more on the defacto premise of **Payment of Value Given to Maximize Company Profit.**

With that change, it forced a slew of complications that came with the unending advance of technology to offer new ways to increase our "quality of living" simply by buying lots of stuff.

I have suggested that the *true purpose* and only purpose of money is intrinsically tied together with *two parts* which can be

## 14 The True Purpose of Money

thought of as a (bi-directional movement of funds from one type of account to another).

**Part A** is called **compensation in Wages for useful work** that most people should be able to assume is intended **for the benefit of the Common Good.**

Sadly, Part A now seems to fall into a new way of looking at money as simply wages received by the workers for helping to maintain company profits no matter which company they are working for which is apparently irrelevant to the question of how much good that "useful work" has helped Society in general.

**Part B** is to offer part of one's personal Wages as payment **to accomplish credit-clearing** in response to a purchase of a product or a service so that **Value Given for Value Received** will always be maintained.

And sadly, Part B has mostly taken on a new identity called **"Avoiding Default of Payments"** so that the bottom line for personal and business accounts is always mandated to stay above zero, or punishment from the higher-ups will ensue to determine what kind of punitive action is to be taken (justified or not).

In other words, a "cast-in-diamond rule of finance ensures that **no dropping below zero** of any type of account balance will ever go unpunished.

Another rule of all present monetary systems in the world is that all **purposeful acquisitions of unearned money** are either called a crime or "good business" depending on who is involved in giving their (worldview opinion.

If Part B was maintained simply as Payment for Products or Services received aka Credit-Clearing to ensure **Value Given for Value Received**, it would have retained its purpose and fulfilled its intent without dragging punitive thinking into the process.

Thinking of money **only as the premise** of **Value Given for Value Received** for the **benefit of the Common Good** would be the powerful change and simplification that is long over-due for humanity on this planet.

For the nations of the world and the "wealthy elite" to **sync their thoughts** to this end has been soundly disparaged and even declared undesirable because other purposes for money by those

## 14 The True Purpose of Money

who have more than they need to start with can easily conjure up *a slew of legal maneuvers to avoid fair play*.

Not only do the *other purposes* for money (like a cancer) become easily manifested as a *malignant form of energy* that goes directly against the Value for Values premise, but they also tend to reduce the efficiency of the entire Global Economy by taking *money out of the equation for a healthy Economy*, to force it out of circulation so it can be used for personal-gain purposes by those (always) at the top.

Going against the efficiency and quality of life factors originally intended, modern thoughts about money often tend to generate *stress, fears and worries about bills being paid on time, accounts being overdrawn*, and simply not having funds to pay for subsistence supplies deemed essential in households the world over.

In most present-day nations and cultures, concerns about money have taken on some bizarre notions that are so far from the original purpose that *personal energies dealing with money* are becoming an *obsession* in our daily routine.

Nowadays, money issues seem to be the *universal trigger* for conflict, hatred, tyranny and wars that end up taking the lives of significant portions of the world's population, past present and foreseeable future with *no end in sight*.

At present, there seems to be *no visible way to stop this* except in the minds of those with a vision for the future as it always has been, is and always will be.

Sadly, many *visions for greatness* have fallen far short of *realistic goals* to make significant changes to the apparently unchangeable equation of money control by the wealthy.

It is still a *constant battle of the wealthy* pitted against most of the middle and poor class folks that are seemingly always held in financial slavery.

*Most are held in unsatisfactory occupations that are not in their best interests, nor are they the best fit for their talents or choices for fulfillment in life.*

Instead, *forced accountability of money* has generated a slavery of oppression upon the 99% lower financial status out of sheer *desperation to survive*.

One of the presently accepted "purposes" of money that would not be permitted in the SANE Economy is to allow some people to *sue for ridiculous amounts* that seem clearly a ruse to get easily obtained unearned settlement by pursuing some issue they *always perceive* is the other party's fault.

These situations generally must be sorted out legally and more equitably by using *additional money* to settle issues that should be handled with a cooperative and intelligent approach by all parties in contention.

When talking about monetary accountability, there are two sides of the coin (pun intended), the first being the *mandated accountability* for every man, woman and child to handle money legally by always paying their bills and never allowing their bank accounts to go negative.

This means there are *virtually no exceptions to the rule allowed* regardless of affordability or good intentions offered with respect to forced accountability to pay for necessities.

Monetary infringements tend to be *brutally pounced upon* and called various names such as counterfeiting, robbery, burglary, fraud, embezzlement, blackmail, etc.

**But what about the other side of the coin,** namely financial accountability of those who are given *free rein to act fraudulently and still stay within the law?*

Why are there so many in business and government who can *amass unearned wealth legally* and not be accountable until they are voted out of office, or replaced in management?

Consider some situations where money is being flagrantly misused, and how *ShareFlow and the SANE Economy* would remedy the situation.

A few examples of answers to the question of "*What is the true purpose of money?* are stated as follows:

One situation affecting untold millions is where many low-income families are forced to scrape or beg just for survival.

# 14 The True Purpose of Money

Forcing many normally responsible folks to scrape for a living is not the true purpose of money since it keeps them in an endless scramble for more income to make two-ends meet.

**Telling them to get a decent job does not compute, since those "decent jobs" are hardly available to the low-income folks due to circumstances making it difficult or impossible to break free and get the education they need.**

And often those "good jobs" may not even exist due to management priorities that cannot invest in them or refuse to create in favor of greater company profit.

Many times, painful choices must be made regarding what folks can afford such as **either adequate healthcare or purchasing good food** for a healthy diet.

Both choices affect their well-being and whether they can even be **healthy enough** to succeed at their job.

Often, necessary education is not always available due to the priority of income going to maintaining subsistence while trying to get **education** to qualify for adequate employment.

This is a situation where our modern monetary system and technology could cooperate to change the equation but priority for company profits always gets in the way.

In other words, **company profit always comes first**, and the welfare of society is a distant second and may not even be considered when **employee salaries are set and not applied in relation to employee worth**.

ShareFlow would provide a straight-forward solution to all these difficulties and more.

By doing so it would define one of the real purposes money is needed in any sensible and civilized mode of operation.

By working with and supporting **only 100% Non-Profit operations**, it would disable all opportunities for profit and pay all workers **directly and adequately** by their Local Banks.

Each Local Bank would be owned and managed **by the Account Holders themselves** so that their families do not have to make these kinds of painful choices.

## 14 The True Purpose of Money

Another common example of money gone awry is the woeful inadequacy of our healthcare industry and medical field to keep costs affordable to all.

Keeping costs affordable only to a relatively few is not the true purpose of money, since medical costs in the United States and other regimes *dominated by conservative thinking* are so far not able to change the equation.

Once again, the *not-so-subtle culprit is profit* and often outrageous profits as in prescription drugs, medical equipment manufacturing, facilities and education to train doctors and nurses and specialists to handle equipment and procedures.

How would ShareFlow and the SANE Economy eliminate the high costs that often force such difficult choices?

It all comes down to ShareFlow with a Network of Local Banks owned and managed by the Banks' customers to where *profit is eliminated* from the economic spectrum.

Furthermore, all reliable Workers are paid directly by their Local Banks so that *adequate and sustainable incomes* are maintained for all no matter how they contribute.

Since ShareFlow would *create all the money when needed* within the Local Banking Network, there would be *no need for profit of any kind by anyone*, and there would be *no need for taxes to be paid by anyone either* at any level thus eliminating the need for the IRS, the Federal Reserve, the Stock Market, the investment companies and any other facility concerned with balanced budgets, debt or profit.

A few examples of financial malaise and misuse contrasted with the antidote that spells out clearly what the real purpose of money should be and how it would correct the situations are described as follows:

Consider some years ago when food companies suddenly became required to go to often extraordinary means to protect packaged foods, bottles and drinks because of some *publicized incidents* where public safety was compromised.

Why did the food companies have to go to such extreme means to add inconvenient capping and wrapping to protect the public from product tampering?

# 14 The True Purpose of Money

The FDA forced mass recalls and shutdown unless at-risk packaged foods were rendered tamper-proof out of concern for public health and safety.

However, it seems obvious to many that food companies claiming to prioritize prevention of harm to the public have another reason for responding so quickly.

Due to the profit motive being company priority, **the fear of getting shut down** was apparently the real driving force.

The future antidote: ShareFlow will automatically provide a simple solution by **paying virtually all Workers of any company supported by the Network** adequate money in Wages so they don't have as much incentive to think they can get easy money with an individual or class-action suit.

Most importantly, ShareFlow would pay all Wage earners **sufficiently** for yet another reason.

That would be to allow them adequate time for training at home to teach their children the way to have **a great quality of life** without trying to hurt others and strive for easy money.

In other words, ShareFlow would take away **many of the incentives** to cheat others by providing **quality of life** for all.

An example of frivolous or unnecessary law-suits that illustrates a similar problem and solution is when home owners are mandated to shovel their walks of snow and ice or face the possibilities of a **law suit** if someone is injured on the walkway.

Common sense says that most people are willing to clear their walkways when able to do so, but when it becomes mandated, it adds an **ominous threat** to the situation.

No one likes being **forced to do the right thing** if the **incentive to shirk responsibility** is taken away.

Some are elderly or handicapped and cannot clear their walkways immediately, but **acting in fear of a lawsuit**, they may put themselves in danger of a fall or a heart attack if they must comply when doing so puts them danger.

Solution: **ShareFlow and SANE would pay all Wage earners and the handicapped adequately** to take away the **incentives for easy money in a law suit** and handle all costs of caring for the injured whenever necessary.

## 14 The True Purpose of Money

*SANE* would provide adequate insurance available to pay for all injuries or even deaths to make it totally unnecessary for anyone to file a lawsuit.

A final example: The ***HIPAA Privacy Rule*** also known as ***The Standards for the Privacy of Individually Identifiable Health Information*** is a Law that establishes a set of national standards for the protection of certain health information accessible by medical personnel ***to not give*** health information to anyone other than the patients or their families regarding any treatment or health records of those being treated.

This is a clear case of where ***Fear of Law Suits*** involving the divulgence of patient privacy information ***becomes way more important than the advertised concern*** of so-called ***privacy protection*** of the patients.

In some cases, this Law has the potential to do more harm than good by withholding important knowledge instead of using ***common sense criteria*** that was acceptable years ago.

The Solution: > Let *SANE* take care of the "harm" that privacy divulgence allegedly occurs so it could abolish the HIPPA Law entirely to allow proper education and ***common sense*** in cases where ***important higher truth*** should prevail.

Bottom line: ***Money is not supposed to be used as a weapon to batter people into submission*** just to protect their ***anything*** when ***common sense could prevail*** within an Economy run by ShareFlow and SANE that could generate permanent solutions ***without so many mandates***.

# ~15~
# A Universal Monetary System

Consider all the national and regional currency systems in existence that will likely want to resist and defy change to their way of doing business.

All the major players (the U.S., Russia, Europe, China, Japan, India, etc. might be stunned if they knew there was a serious contender, a credible challenge offering a formidable difference to the way they think about money.

They may take a dim view *in the way ShareFlow money via electronic currency is used,* since each of them have their own standard of currency they think is working quite well.

I think they would be hard pressed to accept the idea that a sensible currency could go universal and take over the entire global economic mechanics to eventually brush aside all their hard fixed, government-controlled systems and send them into the realm of irrelevancy.

All the major players have established systems of currency that might be severely challenged (or legally stymied) to make a *changeover to a Global Cooperative of Local Banks* that would replace all other currency with exclusive use of *self-created electronic money* as a global standard.

Fortunately, one of the *weapons against resistance* of this nature is the Internet or a similar media that could connect the world for *potentially cooperative capabilities.*

But is it really such a huge stretch of the imagination that *this idea now only considered a dream could become a reality* called The Socially Adapted Network Economy (A SANE Economy powered by ShareFlow, a Network of Local Banks that would be designed to eventually evolve into a *Universal Monetary System* that would work well for all people no matter what their station in life may be?

# 15 A Universal Monetary System

Any global economy with the word "SANE" attached to it would have to be closely aligned with the equivalent of a ShareFlow philosophy by simply having only **one cooperative standard** to replace the inefficient competition of nations for sensible currency everywhere.

I call it Sharo Electronic Currency to eventually phase out all existing currencies by **transitioning existing funds of equal value** into Sharo Units for all Account Holders no matter what standard they would currently be using.

I see a shift in thinking about money as the driving force behind a **sensible change,** whose time is overdue.

Reasons for this include the complexities of modern living, the advances in technology and gradual acceptance of greater racial tolerance as a practical means of living.

A sensible **One-World Currency** would be a huge step forward for humanity where the **usual pragmatism and unusual ethics** come together to support a practical way to create and sustain the things we most want and need in life.

**OWC *would guide us all along a new path leading to greater peace, joy, comfort, quality of values, fulfillment of our purpose and fruition of our fondest dreams.***

Electronic currency is the technological reality that makes a one-world currency not only possible, but credibly sensible across a wide spectrum of philosophical thinking.

It is obvious to many that the physical handling of money in the traditional sense causes stress, takes up too much time and opens the door to greater fraud and illegal acquisition and control of money that is now so apparent in virtually every financial standard the world over.

This is especially true and a no-brainer in the minds of most sensible thinkers that there are **too many other things in life** most practical folks would rather attend to.

Electronic currency is the alternate energy for a **universal standard** that makes good sense in so many ways that any attempts to stop it now seems like sheer nonsense to those who have the greater perspective.

# 15 A Universal Monetary System

It would be akin to trying to stop an avalanche of mud and rocks after the first huge boulder has already triggered and sent a much larger slide on the way down.

A truly efficient Global Money Standard speaks out clearly at a high level of truth to those who think it through carefully.

It is *gaining ground even if the gains are subtle* and hard for most casual thinkers to detect.

They cannot detect changes if they only accept the media of social and political truths as their filter for credibility and worthiness for public discussion.

A *Universal Money Standard* is an inevitable plateau that will be reached eventually because status-quo-alternatives to the idea are displaying increasing frustration over the inability of traditional currencies to form any kind of workable equation for greater cooperation in world trade.

Details describing many of the world's standards of currencies are too complicated to mention and far beyond the scope of this book.

Anyone who wants to get a rough idea of just how many currencies are in use today just needs to look up Currency Standards on the Internet.

*It still seems amazing that so many countries have chosen to favor competition instead of cooperation for handling trade and credit clearing responsibilities.*

Even digital currencies that are trying to eliminate the border to border conversion processes for using virtual money in peer to peer exchanges like bitcoin are quite popular as a growing trend but have flaws that leave them in the dust of all serious attempts to *unite the world for mutual benefit to all.*

One notable problem is that they cannot guarantee holding their value, and even worse may be subject to total collapse like anything else on the stock market if public confidence fails.

Of the approximately 200 different currency standards existing as of 2004, I simply list only the Top 10 to make a point about the inefficiencies that just these major standards inherently produce and force upon their citizens.

And it's all because of two driving forces...

## 15 A Universal Monetary System

The first driving force is *fear that another country's standard cannot be trusted*.

The second is the ever-so-present **Profit Motive** to satisfy *corporate greed* for personal gain in investment games.

Traditional money is generally characterized by central control management and pursuit, where each version is subject to a certain amount of mistrust by other individuals, businesses and other country governments in comparison to their own standards, which may also become suspect.

<u>The Top 10 Rated Paper Currency Standards of 2004</u>

The U.S. Dollar
The European Euro
The Japanese Yen
The English Pound Sterling
The Swiss Franc
The Australian Aussie
The Canadian Dollar
The Swedish Crown
The Hong Kong Dollar
The Norway Corona

I recently obtained this list from the Internet, which is a prime example of conditions subject to change.

These currencies are subject to many variables such as world conditions, stock markets, and the major controlling interests in the money supplies.

The totality of variables is numerous and may be trending to greater popularity because of digital currency powered by advanced technology, greed for personal profit, mistrust, and a *mindset for competition rather than cooperation*.

All this plays into the two powerful negative driving forces working together, namely *fear of loss & promise of gain*.

It strikes fear in the average investor due to the roller coaster of huge profits exchanging position with risks of losing

## 15 A Universal Monetary System

values, such that if one wants a ***stable system that works for everyone***, that vision is nowhere in sight yet*, or is it?*

Trying to give a comprehensive history of even the Top 10 World Paper Currencies might be a mind-boggling effort not to mention boring to the average reader.

To make a very long story relatively short and to the point let us consider just a few noteworthy ***problems concerning competitive currencies.***

For travelers the world over, the inconvenience of having to convert one currency to another for the sake of legalities is often bothersome at best.

The obvious concern for many infrequent travelers who wish to spend some money for a vacation and a peaceful getaway from the everyday world of competition is usually a bit time-consuming and not a pleasant task at all.

This is especially true when they are first-time travelers to a country and not sure of the value-for-value exchange from their country to the other plus the reverse conversion for their left-over spending currency on their trip home.

Inconveniences aside, the simple observation that all these currencies (including the digital ones already in existence) are volatile, always in competition and always subject to change and centralized control.

Since there is relatively little standardization among nations to create fixed values and automated standards of conversion, there are not many user-friendly options for ordinary travelers who use only small amounts of money to pay for purchases.

Vacations aside, the need to have simple accounting to keep track of wages, salaries and negate the stress of worrying about having enough money for an acceptable quality of life let alone a memorable vacation.

The luxury of having a united-world currency that is not controlled by the so-called New World Order or any other stigma of self-anointed money-changers in the Temple of the all-mighty Dollar is not only in sight but has been offered in logical theory and credible construct in this short presentation you have been reading.

# 15 A Universal Monetary System

A unique Constitution called SANECon can be the guiding light devoted entirely to ShareFlow management and SANE economic operations.

ShareFlow and SANE working together as one with the SANECon Constitution could set the pace for unprecedented changes to dismantle the New World Order as perceived by many while it shows the right path to a ***benevolent dream*** of fulfillment as it offers a more optimum quality of life for all.

By doing so, it would ***secure the personal rights and freedoms justifiable to all*** plus give full commitment to the standard of ***Value Given for Value Received*** for every financial transaction.

All policies could be ***voted on and approved of*** by Local Bank Account Holders including you and me and be strictly followed at all Local Banks of the ShareFlow Network.

The future goal of establishing the ***Universal Monetary System of sensible economics*** will then be launched as a fulfillment for an idea whose time has surely arrived.

# ~16~
# The Self-Construct Economy

A self-construct economy is any systematic model of doing business that is always operating in a self-maintenance mode and has the means to auto-correct any deficiencies that hinder operation or progress.

To work well, it would have some built-in means of correcting deficiencies *gradually and systematically* by the dynamics that affect over-all beneficial change.

With respect to government, politics and other social concerns, it must *do so without forced or targeted efforts* on the part of outside forces such as activists, forced new laws or any political intervention that appears artificial, intrusive or obviously non-holistic in comparison.

The *non-holistic aspect* is pictured as something that might *seem to correct a problem*, but in doing so often tends to create one or more new problems or be only a *partial or unsatisfactory solution* that doesn't address the core issues.

Any type of self-correcting influence these days seems hard to come by in a world *obsessed with the quest for money*.

Indeed, it is a constant struggle to fill subsistence-disparity gaps because of *political, corporate and media dominance* that apparently wants to steer the masses into focusing only on **financially-based issues that never have a solution.**

Fortunately, there seems to be a new generation of young folks coming on-board that are more willing to exercise *good sense and retain a greater hold on sound judgment* rather than adhering to a legalese mentality of rigid laws and rules.

Many of these laws (sensible or not) can be considered archaic but based mostly on the *overriding fear of punitive action when we don't comply with the rules of the money*

## 16 The Self-Construct Economy

*game invented by those who have set up constraints* to support their ignorance and political control of the masses.

The good news is however, that some seem willing to *just say no to the fear* of bending the rules a bit for problems that *could best be solved with a common-sense approach.*

More sensible thinkers who would more than welcome a *change in dynamics* are now more likely to be coming on-board when dealing with problems of a societal nature

Many seem willing to lend their support to a *makeover of the economic equation* that drives most of our everyday existence with a no-nonsense approach to the issues of life that drive personal energy and focus for a better way of living.

By demonstrating the beginnings of a *saner way of doing business* such as taking a serious look at *SANE and the ShareFlow Electronic Currency System,* the reality of a visible Self-Correcting Influence would more likely be born to form the basis of education given to many others who *also want to come on-board and affect the change.*

The hypothetical startup of the First Local Bank in a *user-friendly environment* that displays the gamut of all features of the SANE Economic Model as defined by the *SANECon Constitution* would thus define the basis for an enormous step forward in human justice.

If faced with brutal opposition to stop such a venture, *this economic model* could not forever be ignored, much to the chagrin of the money bullies who would like to snuff out the whole idea due to fear of doing business *without profit* that their mindset says they must have above all else.

With effective public education to take the place *of profit-oriented brain-washing that promotes sales of every slot gadget under the sun*, the actual effects of a self-correcting influence that is both visible and predictable could soon be offered in an easily understood way for all ages.

Actual improvement in the *quality of life* can start with the Goal of *100% Renewable Clean Energy* to begin the global transformation process away from fossil fuel reliance to a healthier environment for all.

# 16 The Self-Construct Economy

*Trusted income* even more secure than Social Security, Medicare and Medicaid is the promise of the ShareFlow System by operating within a **window of capped maximum and minimums** that work equally well for all.

The SANECon Constitution would be adhered to and be advertised as a major player to set the pace for an *economic self-correcting philosophy* that already is showing evidence of corrective changes.

Still there will always be the trolls who will resist beneficial change due to a *pervading ignorance and ego-based hatred* against anything that looks like a threat to their grip on profit-based ways of doing things.

Some resistance is *inevitable* to planned self-constructing measures, **but not insurmountable** since **beneficial changes** taking place **would also benefit them.**

These benefits would enhance their personal physical and mental comfort zone as well as their need for highly reliable security measures such that they could minimize concerns and anxieties over what the others might do to upset their personal profit-based financial nirvana.

*Adequate education* could *obliterate any suggestions* of doubt about oncoming improvements in the standards of living for humanity because of a clearly observable system we **could resonate with called the Self-Construct Economy.**

From the last chapter we learn that the *miasma of world currencies* presents a dilemma of confusion to many because of mutual mistrust of nations and cultures that have relied only upon their own currencies as a standard.

Now there are so many *standard currencies* that the word *standard* no longer fits the equation.

It seems more appropriate to use the word *competing* to describe the mix appropriately.

But in all due respect, there is another reason why there are so many monetary standards in the world.

That is because of the lack of willingness (or funds) to form a **well-designed universal language** that could help bring opposing cultures together in a spirit of universal cooperation

# 16 The Self-Construct Economy

*rather than maintaining the universal and debilitating mindset of necessary competition.*

The situation can be traced to pragmatism regarding short-term monetary gain as the *universal human trait culprit that seems all too natural to try to oppose it*.

Apparently, there's a self-interest well in place to dominate over all attempts to think clearly in terms of higher truth.

Truly, it's the wealth of the money controllers that takes the reins to force compliance within a system of *confusing legalities that brush aside common sense and many of the basic rights* of ordinary citizens in the process.

Although ShareFlow can start with only one Local Bank to prove itself worthy to ordinary citizens, that Bank alone could be the *trigger* for the right to create their own money and use that money as it was originally intended as *strictly adhering to a Value Given for Value Received philosophy* for Wages and Pricing of all Products and Services.

With ordinary citizens using their well-earned income to purchase all their necessities for their own well-defined and reasonably set *quality of life* for themselves and their families, it bodes the question of how does *the self-construct aspect* of the Economy come into the equation?

A well-planned Self-Construct Economy becomes possible when a *Universal Monetary System is enabled, secure and protected* by an Internal ShareFlow and SANE Constitution called **SANECon** that would guarantee *all Local Control by the Customers of the Local Banks*.

**SANECon** must guarantee that no interference from any *centralized authority or government* can step in to override the process and thus would never be allowed to change it.

One momentous side-effect of the **Universal Monetary System** could possibly be a trigger needed to inspire a *generic and well-thought-out Universal Language* for eventual use by everyone on the planet.

The UL would not have to do away with all other languages but could be used in conjunction with ShareFlow and SANE

# 16 The Self-Construct Economy

to help make business dealings *significantly more efficient based upon cooperation* instead of competition.

Values of all existing standards of money could be converted to the ShareFlow System when the time is right.

Right now, the *time being right* may depend upon when a *critical mass of participants* realize it is crucial to survival.

There are countless variables that are destined to play out when the ***SANE Economy using the ShareFlow Monetary System*** becomes a visible reality.

It will likely garner the attention of the major players of nations throughout the world including the media, the wealthy elite and the politics-as-usual crowds in government that have traditionally controlled *global economic ebb and flow*.

Consider how a Self-Construct Economy would become a major player by becoming a visible self-constructive influence whenever significant problem are identified tending to degrade quality of life for the average citizen.

***Built on the foundation of a benevolent self-control influence precisely specified in SANECon, every person having an Account in their Local Bank will have their shareholder vote to help direct all resources in the global work force to respond to priority needs 24/7.***

Consider a few simple examples:

I as the author of this book wear *contact lenses* and have done so for most of my life.

I have tried virtually all the lens types that exist, and even worked for the ***Mueller Welt Contact Lens Company*** in Chicago part time back in the 50's.

I helped prepare standardized hard plastic "buttons" for lenses with their initial curvatures carved out by machine for processing that resulted in the final product for customers.

To make a long story short, I am now in my 80's and love to wear the latest daily disposable water permeable lenses for three important reasons: namely excellent vision, comfortable wearing and affordability for myself and others.

Some companies are finally realizing that even the best lenses need to be affordable for the average user.

## 16 The Self-Construct Economy

For years, the companies that produced these products have done well on the first two factors but failed badly on the affordability part.

Even though companies are getting the message that affordability IS a vital and necessary factor, the problem still exists for millions of others who cannot even afford an eye exam, let alone the products to correct the problems.

With the SANE Economy and ShareFlow guiding the world's economic stage to better days ahead, the factor of affordability would no longer be a problem for anyone.

The solution is obvious: SANE would automatically create enough money in Sharos to pay for the *necessary education to train workers* who produce contact lenses and other medical items of necessity.

They would do so allowing *only the best materials and techniques for production and distribution be affordable* for the average patient.

With ShareFlow and SANE, the costs of lenses today could be significantly reduced because *all workers involved in the process* would be paid by a ShareFlow Local Bank.

*The Banks would create whatever money is needed for the SANE Policy of educating and directing workers to fill in the gaps* at the locations of highest priority.

In other words, since today's contact lenses of all types are seriously inflated in price, the necessary change in policy would be to **increase mass production with standardization** and have all necessary funds used where they do the most good.

In a very similar manner, the *cost of hearing aids*, although improving in quality and somewhat in affordability still has a long way to go for general delivery to the public at a truly affordable cost.

*Affordability for the best products and procedures at this time are hard to come by for most.*

Again, the solution for this problem is straightforward when ShareFlow money for Wages can come onboard to pay all manufacturers and distributors as needed

# 16 The Self-Construct Economy

Regarding any critical-use product in the medical field such as contact lenses or hearing aids, no person should be left out of the equation due to the ***infamous unaffordability issue.***

At the time of this writing, the best hearing aids still cost thousands of dollars even though by simply and intelligently ***abandoning the Profit Motive*** could make them far more affordable so that no one in need is left out.

A third example and a significant one of great concern for many involves ***dentures to replace lost and diseased teeth.***

This is a prime example of how ***profit has come to the forefront*** in the mind of many providers such that the best products and service available have been inherently difficult to obtain due to the ***reluctance of the providers*** to make prices reasonable and affordable to all who need them.

Saying it in another way, ***dental implants are the usual choice for high quality reliable artificial teeth*** that avoids most if not all the usual problems that natural teeth are subject to, but unfortunately the costs for the best implants have been far too high for many to afford.

Since implants can theoretically work for most in need of teeth replacement, perhaps the only factor stopping the general use of reliable dentures is simply the high cost due to a shortage of specialists with a commitment to make them affordable.

ShareFlow and SANE would solve these concerns by paying all dental providers including Dentists, Specialists, Technicians, Assistants, etc. adequate Wages ***to support the quality of life styles they are worthy of,*** plus the money to pay for education to use new technology-driven products and services to support that goal.

Using advanced tools and techniques for quality dental implants that offer the best service should be the goal for all dental service providers.

Affordability would be possible in a winning combination of ***non-profit operations*** using mass production and quality standardization for all essential pieces of equipment

It would make sense for implants that the support people in modern dentistry should be able to deliver the best and most reliable dentures at a lower cost than their profit-supported counterparts charge today.

These examples are typical and represent just a fraction of what could be done in the Medical and Dental Fields alone.

**Let us now consider a few other examples in the realm of Agriculture and the Food Support Industries:**

For years I have spoken about the need to have the **basics of life sustainable and affordable for all.**

In generalized fashion we can all understand that the rigors of Climate Change and the foibles of humanity are making it much more difficult to grow sustainable and true health foods at affordable costs for everyone.

Scarcity of true health-based foods makes those costs soar beyond reach for many when a healthy economy would make them available and affordable for all.

Solution: ShareFlow and the SANE Economy would easily work together to create and allocate enough money as needed for all these essentials to be affordable for everyone.

**Modern technology, mass production and standard support equipment, customized greenhouses and special growing techniques using only Renewable Clean Energy** would make it possible for most if not all food products to be produced abundantly and healthfully at greatly reduced prices.

ShareFlow would create the necessary funds for all of this.

**Let us consider the Problem of Affordable Housing:**

This is a perennial and chronically continuous problem for countless millions who feel they must make numerous **trade-off decisions just to survive financially.**

The problem is that in most locations there are too many people looking for affordable housing where there is scarcity of land, resources and personnel to build mass housing and the resources in these communities to meet their needs.

**With ShareFlow and SANE in operation,** the problems could quickly disappear as long as Nature or human foibles do not cause apocalyptic catastrophes to occur.

# 16 The Self-Construct Economy

SANE would rely upon self-constructive methodology for willing workers to be trained and paid well to use available land and resources to build whatever affordable housing is possible.

Various occupancy ratings would be considered and be **attainable for virtually everyone to lease or own without going into debt or having add-on fees, interest or taxes of any kind to pay.**

SANE would have the capability to match employment with necessary training or for direct hire to build the facilities while ShareFlow steps in with adequate Wages for motivation and incentives to do high-quality workmanship.

**Consider personal vehicles such as cars, pickup trucks and other family-owned transportation** and the initial high costs, mandated interest, insurance, license fees, etc. that are based upon (supposedly) unavoidable expenses.

Or must they always be *unavoidable*?

It is always *profit-mandated motivations* at the root of every business operation that all vehicle manufacturers and distributors must depend upon.

**Abusive money manipulation and profit will no longer be allowed when ShareFlow and the SANE Economy step in to operate at 100% non-profit status.**

All available workers could be redirected for training and relocation if necessary to modularize, standardize and help mass-produce the high-quality homes necessary for owners to lease or own at all levels of affordability.

These are all examples of major evolutionary forces that could easily be at work to begin the *Self-Construct-Economy* that would bring a high quality of life trending for all including the present wealthy controllers of the money.

Countless other examples of an evolutionary trending and ever-increasing sustainability towards a self-constructive force that would inevitably work to benefit everyone would soon *self-correct all the kinks in the machinery* of an existing Economy to change it forever for the better.

And what better Destiny for us than this?

# 16 The Self-Construct Economy

A Final Example:

In *disaster prone areas* of the nation and around the world, SANE and ShareFlow could be set up so that workers looking for better employment could *accept paid training to build mobile homes* to move into place in and around these areas for use prior to a disaster such as in hurricanes, tornados, fires, floods, etc.

They could be used even for long term droughts, famine or floods to *relocate families, loved ones, pets and important possessions to safer locations* either temporarily or be set up by choice as a permanent solution.

A global-based SANE and ShareFlow working together could eventually arrange for all private land to be leased so that all land on Earth would have the status of *public un-owned property* open freely to all.

This my friends is what ShareFlow and the SANE Economy can potentially do *once that First Local Bank is built* and becomes operational with the full commitment of a SANECon Constitution spelled out for all to see.

With a Universal Monetary System, SANECon, SANE and the ShareFlow Global Network in operation, we will have an unstoppable force for the benefit of *everyone on the Planet.*

It can exist and work well together regardless of status, wealth, gender, race or personal philosophy, and rightfully be called the *Self-Construct Economy*, the Socially Automated Network Economy that is owned and operated by many Bank customers around the world (you and I included).

~ The SANE Economy ~

# ABOUT THE AUTHOR

Alan Halverson is 82 years of age and an active pursuer of social justice for all at the time of this publication.

His birth and early years were in Chicago where he first developed a compelling interest in science and mathematics.

He spent two years in the U.S. Army stateside and later completed his college education at Brigham Young University in Provo, Utah with a B.S. Degree in Physics and Mathematics and a job offer at the Naval Observatory in Washington, D.C.

His professional life continued employment at aerospace firms including NASA-Goddard Space Flight Center in Greenbelt, MD and Ball Research Corporation in Boulder CO as a computer programmer.

Alan's philosophy about life eventually evolved from early evangelical church teachings into other religious associations including New Age thinking and the Mormon philosophy.

His present belief system goes beyond all of that in favor of a personal attunement to the concepts of an Afterlife of truth, light and love available to all regardless of affiliation.

He is a firm believer that we as humans on Earth are eternal souls possibly living many lifetimes over various incarnations according to our own choice to gain experience and education.

He knows that the purpose in life is to seek out higher levels of truth and love for sharing the joys of spiritual living with all others on a similar path seeking the greater truth.

Alan identifies as a messenger to the masses to help build a new world of trust and cooperation based upon justice, equality and freedom from the slavery of money and monetary accountability in favor of a new system.

From the simple definition of a SANE Economy that Alan presents, he offers a bold but rational philosophy regarding logical steps that can achieve a global economy releasing us from the limitations of endless money manipulation that our profit-driven gridlock is presently based upon.

# Recommended Reading

**The End of Money**: Toward a New World Economy
    Under the Credit Unit System
    By Darrel W. Kimble
        ISBN: 0972015108

**Moneyfree**: An Idea Whose Time Has Come
    By Alan Halverson
        ISBN: 978-1530640690

**The Seven Virtues of a Free and Equal Society:**
    A Guide to Social Engineering
    By C.L. Stadler
        ISBN: 9781502961556

**The Moneyless Manifesto:**
    Live Well, Live Rich, Live Free
    By Mark Boyle
        ISBN: 978-1-86253-101-5

**Sacred Economics:**
    Money, Gift and Society in the Age of Transition
    By Charles Eisenstein
        ISBN: 978-1-58394-397-7

**Blueprint for a Golden Society:**
    By J.S. Boehme
        ISBN: 1475181892

# For Additional Copies of The SANE Economy

Check for Title and Author for Purchase on Amazon Books

For Additional Information visit:

http://www.starlightpoint.com/books

or Contact the Author by Email at:

hal2128ad@msn.com

The author encourages readers to take the opportunity to go to
www.amazon.com/books/sane economy/
to give an honest customer review
of this presentation.

~

If desired, you may responsibly
copy or quote material
for postings on
Facebook or
Twitter

~ The SANE Economy ~

www.ingramcontent.com/pod-product-compliance
Lightning Source LLC
Chambersburg PA
CBHW050258230526
45471CB00005B/1932